Making Paper Flowers and Decorations

Making Paper Flowers and Decorations

Suzy Ives

Taplinger Publishing Co., Inc.
New York

First published in the United States in 1973 by
TAPLINGER PUBLISHING CO., INC.
New York, New York

Copyright © 1973 by Suzy Ives
All rights reserved
Printed in Great Britain

No part of this publication may be reproduced or
transmitted in any form or by any means,
electronic or mechanical, including photocopy,
recording, or any information storage and
retrieval system now known or to be invented,
without permission in writing from the publisher,
except by a reviewer who wishes to quote brief
passages in connection with a review written for
inclusion in a magazine, newspaper or broadcast.

Library of Congress Catalog Card Number: 73–2325
ISBN 0-8008-5057-2

For John

ACKNOWLEDGMENT

I would like to thank Charlotte Baron for her help
with the photographs and design of this book.
Also Mrs Gwen Ives and Mrs Daphne Rolt for their
assistance with the simple crêpe flower and the
crêpe flower with fringed centre.
And once again, my grateful thanks to
Thelma M. Nye of Batsford for her constant help
and encouragement.

S.J.I.
Teddington 1973

CONTENTS

FOREWORD	9
CRÊPE PAPER FLOWERS	11
Simple crêpe poppy	13
Simple crêpe flower with shaped petals	17
Crêpe flower with padded centre	21
Crêpe flower table decoration	25
Crêpe sunflower	27
Crêpe flower with fringed centre	31
Crêpe bell flower with fringed centre	33
Crêpe flower posy	37
Crêpe flower branch	41
TISSUE PAPER FLOWERS	43
Simple tissue flower	45
Tissue flower quatrefoil	49
Tissue paper cabbage rose	51
Tissue paper rose	55
Tissue flower ball	57
Tissue flower cone	61
CARTRIDGE PAPER FLOWERS	64
Cartridge paper buttercup	65
Cartridge paper daisy	69
Cartridge paper tulip	73
Cartridge paper art deco daisy	77
MIXED PAPER FLOWERS	80
Mixed paper flower 1	81
Mixed paper flower 2	85
WREATHS AND DECORATIONS	86
Christmas wreath	87
Dish arrangement	91
Cornucopia	93
SUPPLIERS	96

FOREWORD

Paper flowers will brighten any room, either as a permanent decoration or for a special occasion arrangement. They are easy to make, simple to arrange and virtually everlasting.

All the flowers in this book are made from paper on a wire or bamboo stem. Paper is such an adaptable medium to work with that many different effects can be achieved from a simple basic form.

There are several tools and materials that are needed for these flowers, the basic tools being common to most of the flowers. The papers used are described at the beginning of each section.

TOOLS

Scissors
These must be sharp and in good condition; there is nothing worse than trying to cut out a smooth shape with blunt and loose scissors.
Three pairs are needed:
A large pair with blades approximately 101 mm (4 in.) long
A smaller pair with pointed tips and blades 25 mm to 37 mm (1 in. to $1\frac{1}{2}$ in.) long
A pair of pinking shears

A pair of pliers
These should have a good grip for bending wire and a cutting attachment between the head and the handle.

Wire
Heavy wire for the stems of the flowers. This is bought by weight. 1·25 mm ($\frac{1}{16}$ in.) wire is suitable. Fuse wire for binding the flower head to the stem.

Split bamboo sticks
These are used as an alternative to wire.

Glue
Rubber solution glue, strong paper glue.

Sticky tape
Transparent cellophane tape and masking tape.

Pins
Long steel pins and hairpins.

Floral arrangement pad and ball   Ribbon
Satin or velvet ribbon about 19 mm ($\frac{3}{4}$ in.) wide.

Also
A soft pencil, rubber and 1 inch squared graph paper.
A blunt knife for scoring card and cartridge paper.
A scalpel or craft knife.

FIRE RISK

With care all these flowers are perfectly safe, but never, never put them near to a fire or on a mantelpiece when a fire is burning. Always make sure that the vase the flowers are in is firm and if it seems unsteady, anchor it by filling the base of the vase with pebbles.

GRAPHS

On all the graphs given in this book, one square represents 25 mm (1 in.) unless otherwise stated.

CREPE PAPER FLOWERS

INTRODUCTION

Crêpe paper is sold in packets, the paper being 2·5 metres (8 ft 6 in.) long and 508 mm (20 in.) wide. The grain of the paper runs across the strip. It is made in a wide range of colours from pale tones to brilliant, vivid colours. Although strong sunlight will fade most colours, crêpe paper seems to be less subject to fading than many other papers.

Crêpe paper is admirably suited to paper flower making because, although it is not thick, it is strong and pliable and can be stretched.

Pay careful attention to the direction of the grain when cutting out these flowers as it makes a tremendous difference to the finished effect.

Simple crêpe poppy

MATERIALS

A piece of thick wire 457 mm (18 in.) long, with 25 mm (1 in.) bent to a right angle at one end
5 amp fuse wire 1·8 m (6 ft)
1 packet scarlet crêpe paper (this will make two flowers)
Large pair of scissors
Pinking shears
Ruler and pencil

Simple crêpe poppy

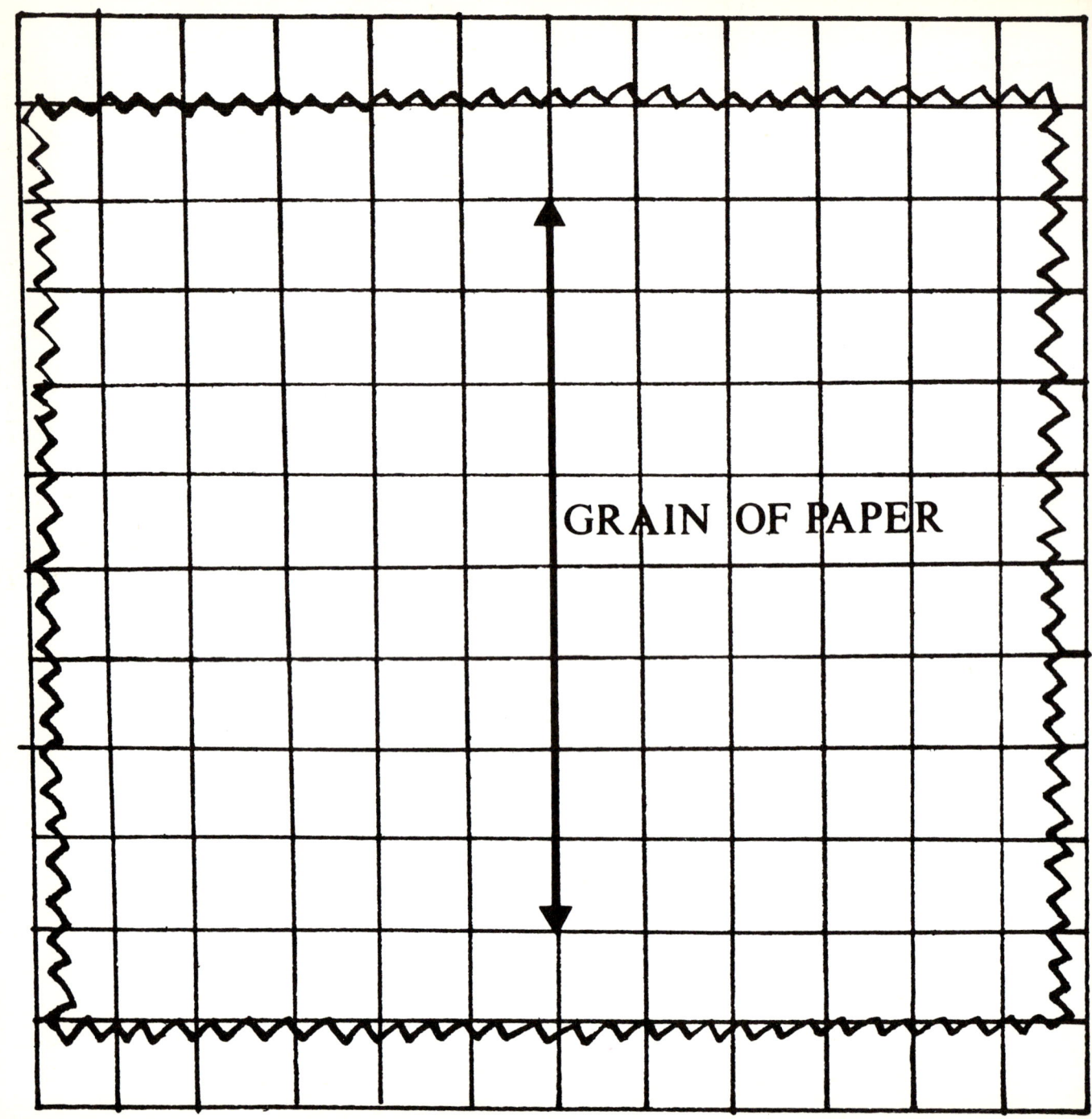

METHOD

Cut the roll of crêpe paper in half and unroll one half. Cut this up into 8 pieces, each piece measuring 304 mm (12 in.) by 254 mm (10 in.) with the grain running parallel to the 254 mm (10 in.) side, see graph.

Trim all the edges with pinking shears.

Place all the paper pieces on top of one another and pleat them up across the middle. Pleat tightly.

Cut the fuse wire into six 304 mm (12 in.) lengths.

Bind the centre of the pleats with three strands of the fuse wire, leaving the ends of the fuse wire free so that they can be used to bind the flower to the stem.

Tease out the layers of pleated crêpe, starting with the uppermost layer. Gently lift and pull the two halves of this layer together and stretch them across the grain.

Do this with all the other layers until the flower head is a globe shape.

Bind the flower head to the stem at the right angle.

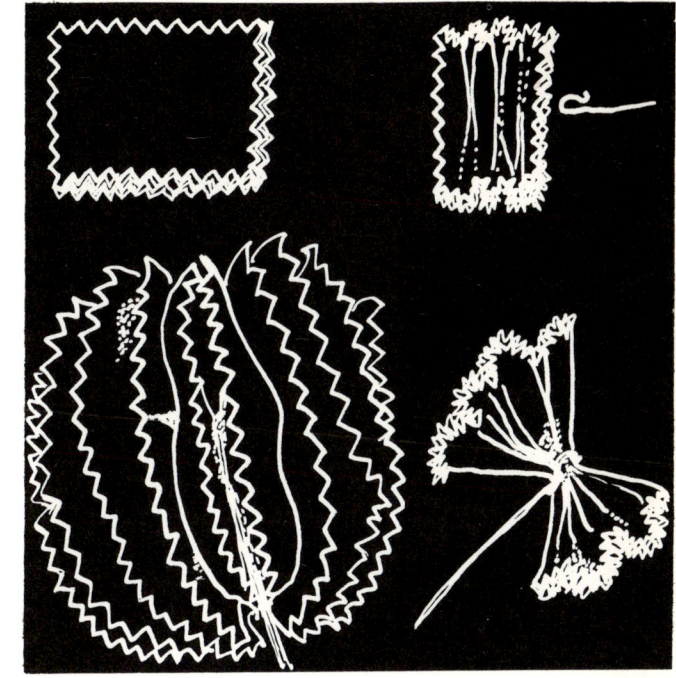

Simple crêpe flower with shaped petals

MATERIALS

A piece of thick wire 431 mm (17 in.) long, or a split
bamboo stick of the same length
Rubber solution glue
Two packets crêpe paper in complementary colours
(this will make two flowers)
Large pair of scissors
Pencil, graph paper 25 mm (1 in.) squares

Simple crêpe flower with shaped petals

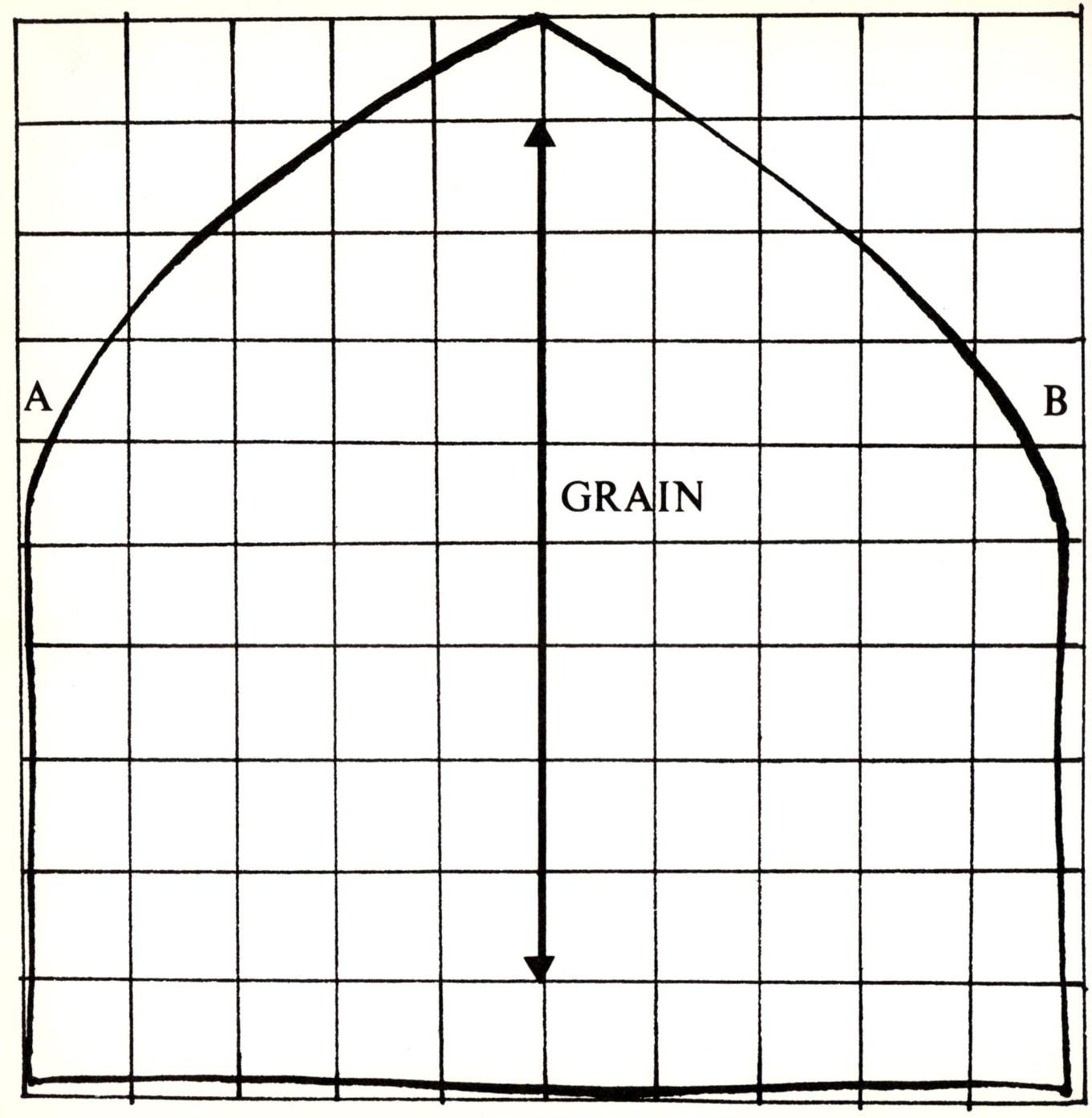

METHOD

Unwind the rolls of crêpe paper and refold them until the roll measures 508 mm (20 in.) long by 254 mm (10 in.) wide.

Cut each roll in half through the middle so that they now measure 254 mm (10 in.) square.

Make a paper pattern from the graph [one square on the graph equals 25 mm (1 in.)]. Using the graph paper shape as a template, cut round it on the crêpe paper, cutting only from A to B, leaving the paper *uncut* at each side.

Unroll the paper petals, they form a strip.

Lay one end of the stem on one edge of the strip of petals. Dab a little glue on the crêpe paper and begin to roll the strip of petals round the stem. Pleat up the base of each petal as it is rolled, gluing as you go. When the first strip of petals is rolled round the stem, glue on the next strip. Stretch the base of each petal gently and carefully, starting with the outside petals and working inwards. This gives the flower a globed shape.

Crêpe flower with padded centre

MATERIALS

A piece of thick wire 431 mm (17 in.) long, or a split bamboo stick of the same length
Rubber solution glue
Two packets of crêpe paper in two shades of the same colour (eg red and deep pink) and small scraps of black crêpe paper
Large pair of scissors
Pencil, tracing paper
A cork
Length of cotton thread

Crêpe flower with padded centre

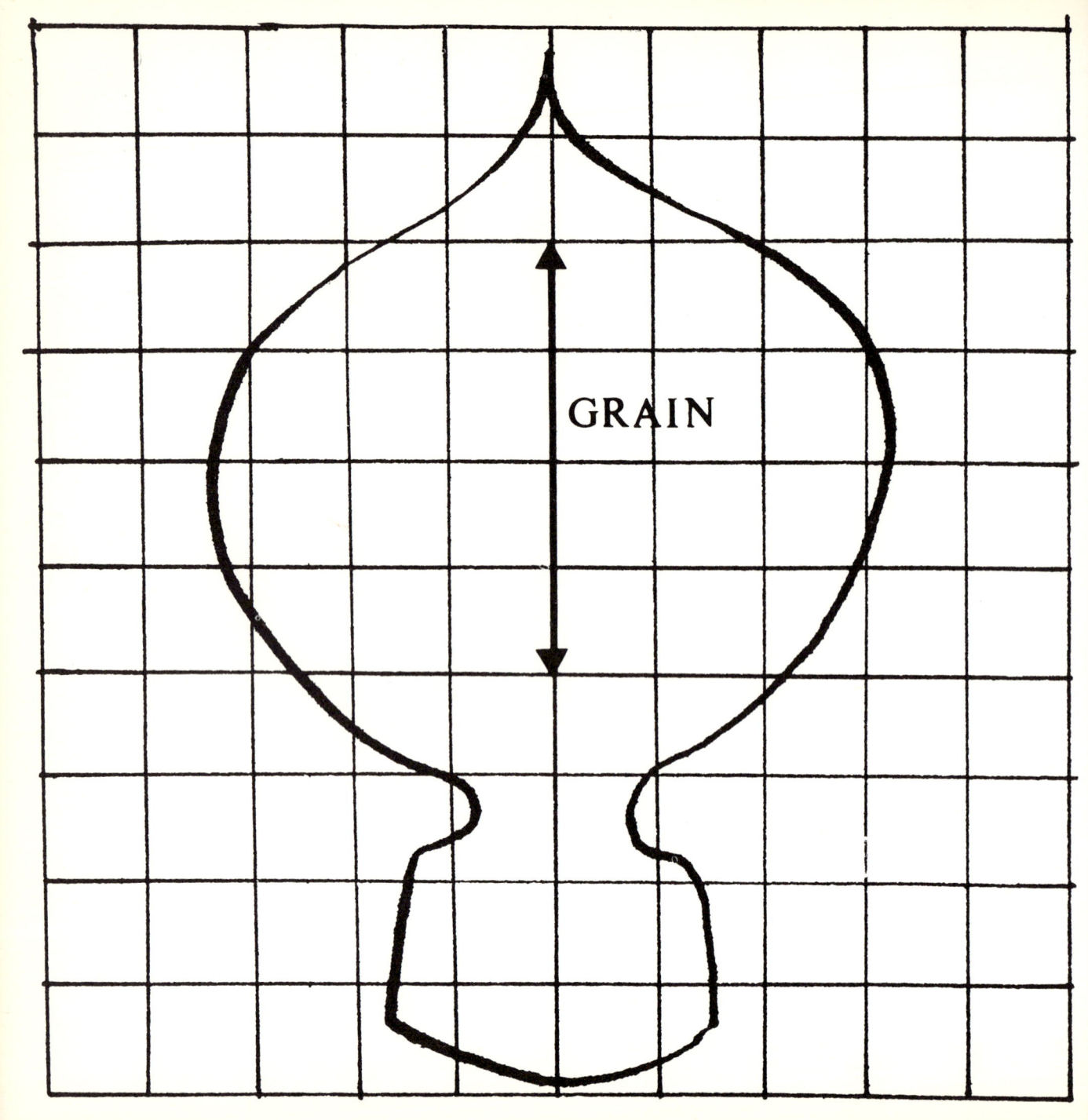

METHOD

Cover the cork with scraps of black crêpe paper, bound in place with a length of cotton thread.
Make the tracing paper pattern direct from the graph.
Using the traced paper pattern as a template, cut out eight petals, four of each colour.
Push the end of the stem into the paper covered cork.
Dab a little glue onto the base of each petal and stick the petals to the stem, just below the cork.
Tease out the petals to give the flower fullness.
Bind the stem with a narrow strip of crêpe paper glued into position.

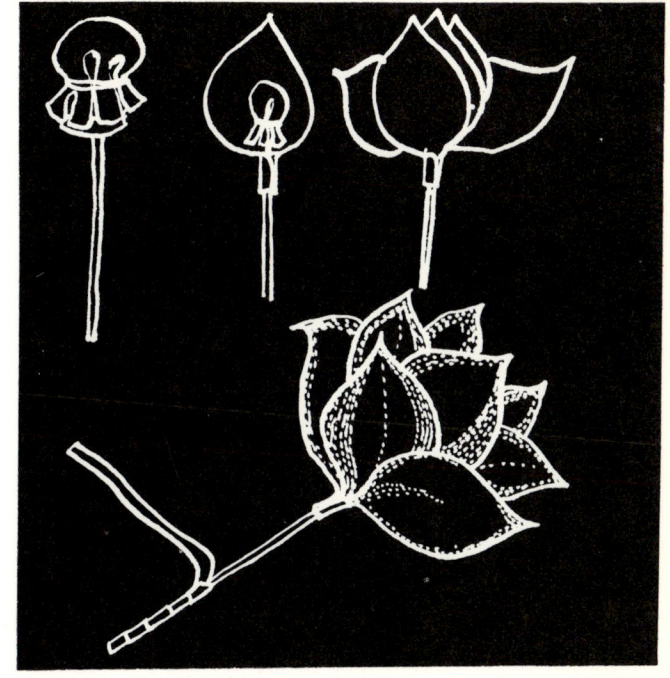

23

Crêpe flower table decoration

MATERIALS

A postcard
Rubber solution glue
Two packets of crêpe paper in complementary colours
Large pair of scissors
Pencil, graph paper 25 mm (1 in.) squares

Crêpe flower table decoration

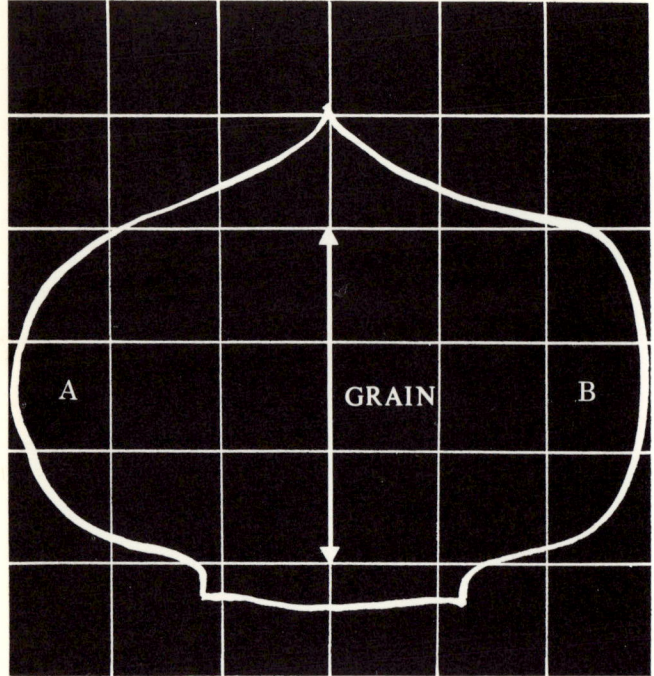

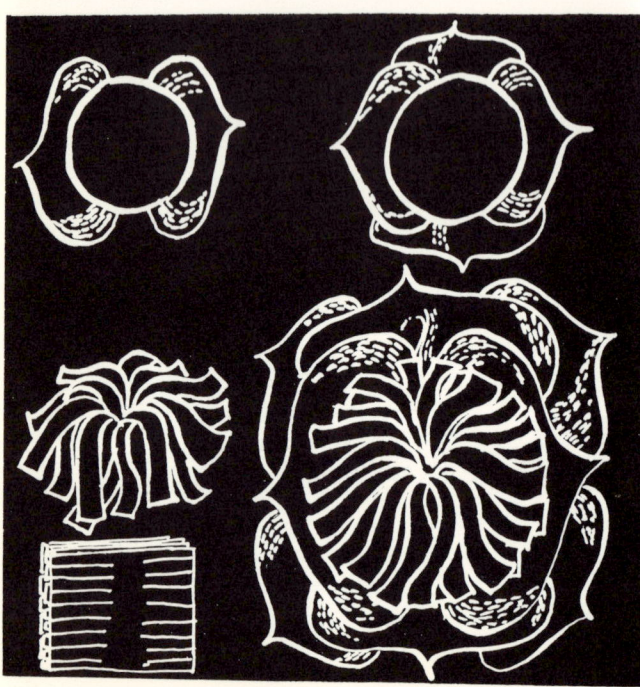

METHOD

Make a paper pattern from the graph [one square on the graph is equal to 25 mm (1 in.)]

Using the graph paper pattern as a template, cut ten petals from one of the packets of crêpe paper.

Stretch each petal between points A and B, leaving the upper point and lower edge unstretched. This will cause the petal to curl up.

Cut a circle from the postcard 76 mm (3 in.) in diameter.

Stick the petals to the circle in pairs so that the petals curl round the card.

From the other packet of crêpe paper cut eight pieces each 127 mm × 101 mm (5 in. × 4 in.).

Snip into the edges of each piece, across the grain.

Stick these fronded pieces of paper to each other, so that the fronds on each layer point in different directions. Pinch the centre so that they bunch up slightly.

Stick the frond into the centre of each flower.

These flowers make very effective table decorations.

Crêpe sunflower

MATERIALS

A piece of thick wire 431 mm (17 in.) long, or a split bamboo stick of the same length
Rubber solution glue
Two packets of crêpe paper, one yellow, one brown
Strip of green crêpe paper 304 mm × 152 mm (12 in. × 6 in.)
Small piece of stiff cardboard 304 mm × 152 mm (12 in. × 6 in.)
Yellow paint
Small scraps of corrugated paper
Scissors, pinking shears and scalpel
A cork
Pencil, graph paper 25 mm (1 in.) squares

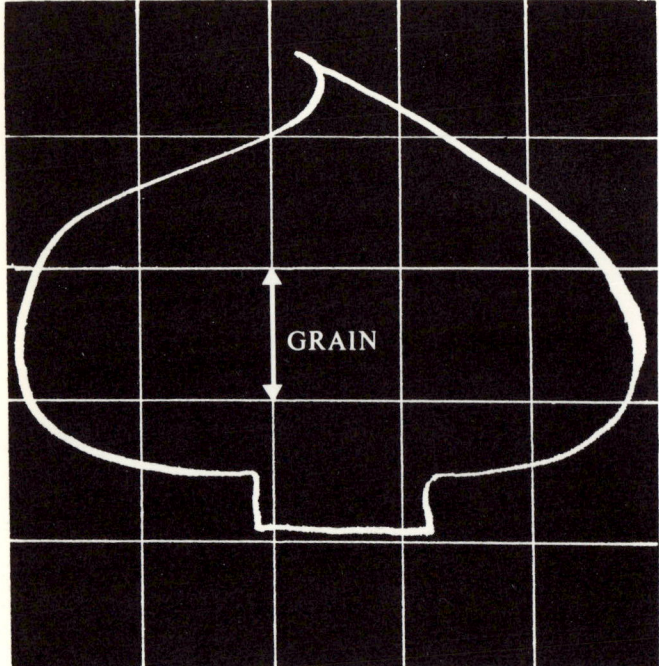

METHOD

Cut two circles from the stiff card, each 152 mm (6 in.) in diameter.

Paint them yellow.

From the scraps of corrugated paper, cut narrow strips about 12 mm ($\frac{1}{2}$ in.) wide.

Roll up these strips and glue the ends down. You will need about twenty.

Glue the rolled up strips of corrugated paper onto one of the cardboard circles.

Make a graph paper pattern from the graph [one square on the graph is equal to 25 mm (1 in.)].

Cut out thirty two petals, from the yellow and brown crêpe paper, using the graph paper pattern as a template.

Stick the petals in overlapping layers onto the underside of the decorated card circle.

Stretch the base of each petal so that it curls up round the card circle.

Stick the second circle onto the back of the first, this will hide the base of the petals.

Cut the cork in half and glue it to the underside of the flower.

Cut a circle 177 mm (7 in.) diameter from the green crêpe using pinking shears, and glue this over the back of the flower so that the cork is concealed.

Drive the end of the stem into the cork.

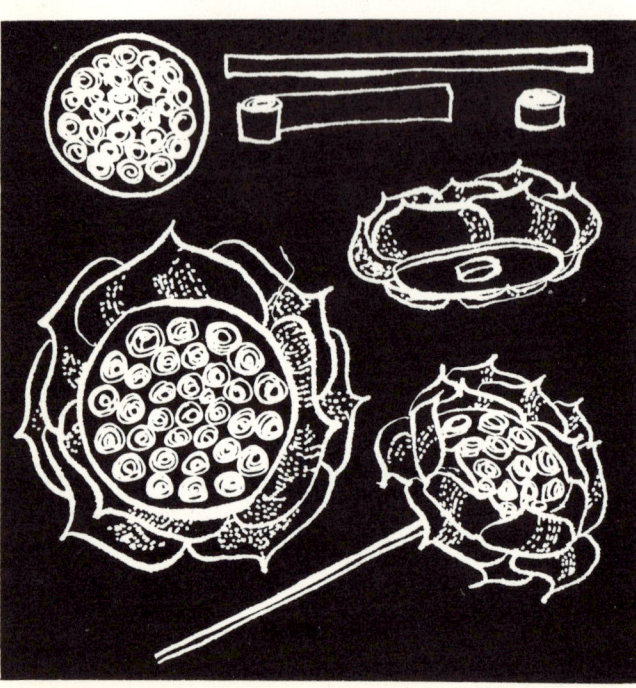

Crêpe sunflower

Crêpe flower with fringed centre

MATERIALS

A piece of thick wire 431 mm (17 in.) long, or a split
bamboo stick of the same length
Rubber solution glue
Three packets of crêpe paper, one in yellow
Large pair of scissors
Pencil, tracing paper

Crêpe flower with fringed centre

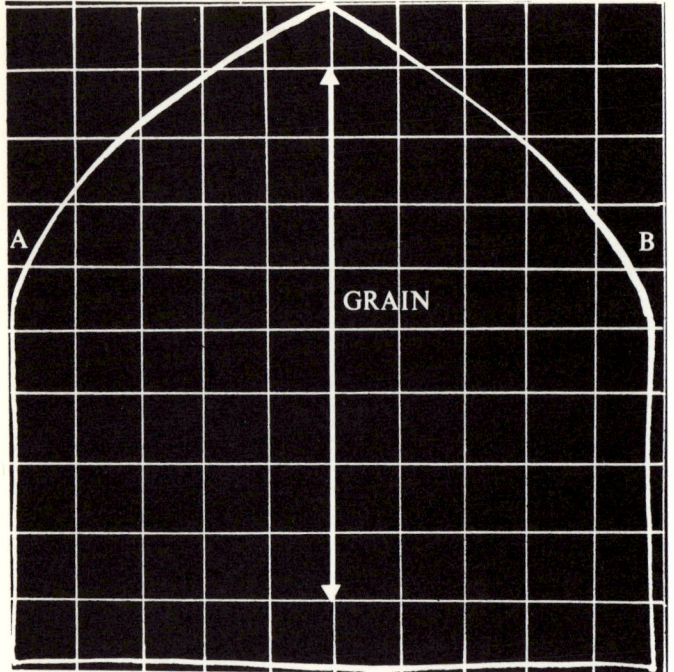

METHOD

Make two strips of petals as in the directions given for the second crêpe paper flower on page 19. Make a graph paper pattern from the graph on page 18. The same graph has been reproduced smaller on this page.

Using the yellow crêpe paper, cut the roll in half to make a strip 254 mm (10 in.) wide and at least 1·2 m (4 ft) long.

Cut into one the edges of this strip (*not* a folded edge) to make a fringe.

Roll the fringed strip tightly round the stem, gluing it in place.

Add two strips of petals as for the flower on page 19 and stretch them as before.

PLATE 1 *(Opposite)*   *Crêpe flower with fringed centre*

Crêpe bell flower with fringed centre

MATERIALS

A piece of medium weight wire 431 mm (17 in.) long, or a split bamboo stick of the same length
Two packets of crêpe paper (these will make several flowers)
Rubber solution glue
Scissors
Masking tape

(Overleaf) Crêpe bell flower with fringed centre

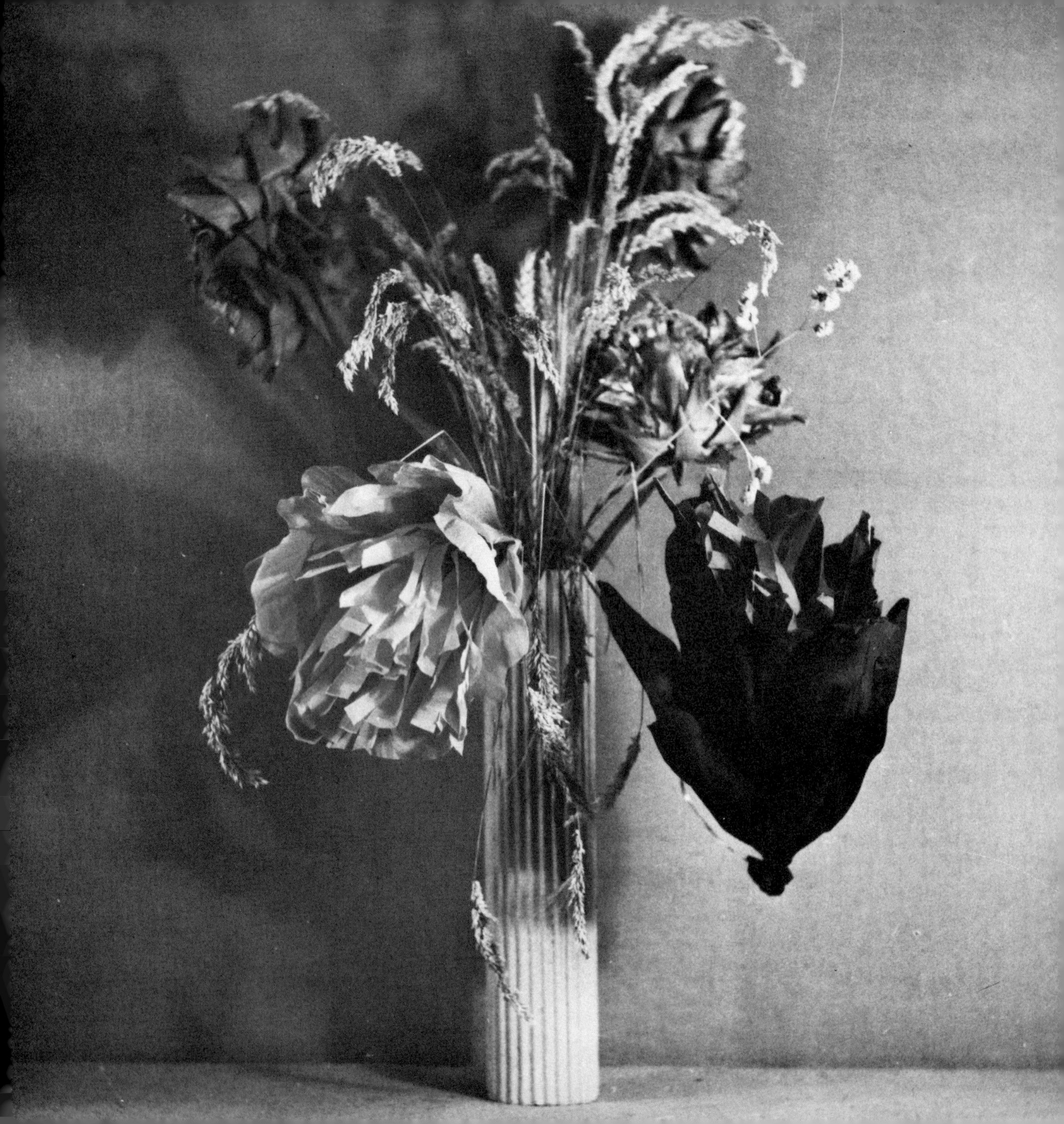

GRAIN

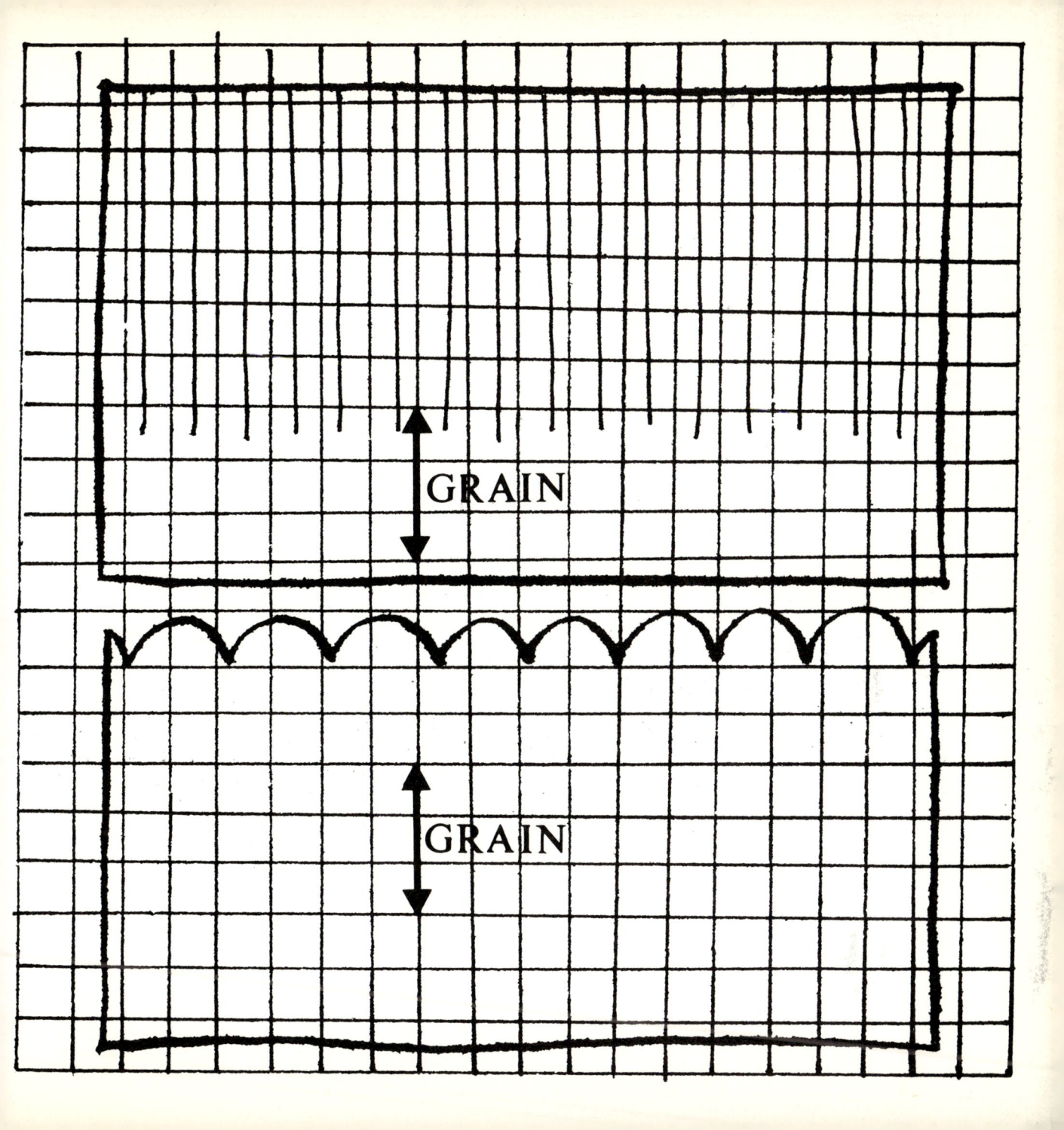

GRAIN

METHOD

Cut each of the packets of crêpe paper into pieces 431 mm (17 in.) long and 254 mm (10 in.) deep.

Cut three strips with a fronded edge and three with a curved edge (see graph).

Wind the three fronded strips tightly round one end of the stem and glue the edge firmly.

Glue the edge of each curved edge strip so that each forms a cylinder.

Slip each cylinder down the stem over the fronded flower centre. Gather the straight edge round the stem and bind with masking tape. The final cylinder should be glued at the stem end so that the masking tape is covered.

Stretch the base of each cylinder slightly to give a belled shape.

These flowers look best when they point down or up, so bend the wire stem about halfway along so that the flowers hang well.

Crêpe flower posy

MATERIALS

Sixteen lengths of medium weight wire, each 406 mm (16 in.)
Two packets of crêpe paper in complementary colours
Paper glue
Scissors

METHOD

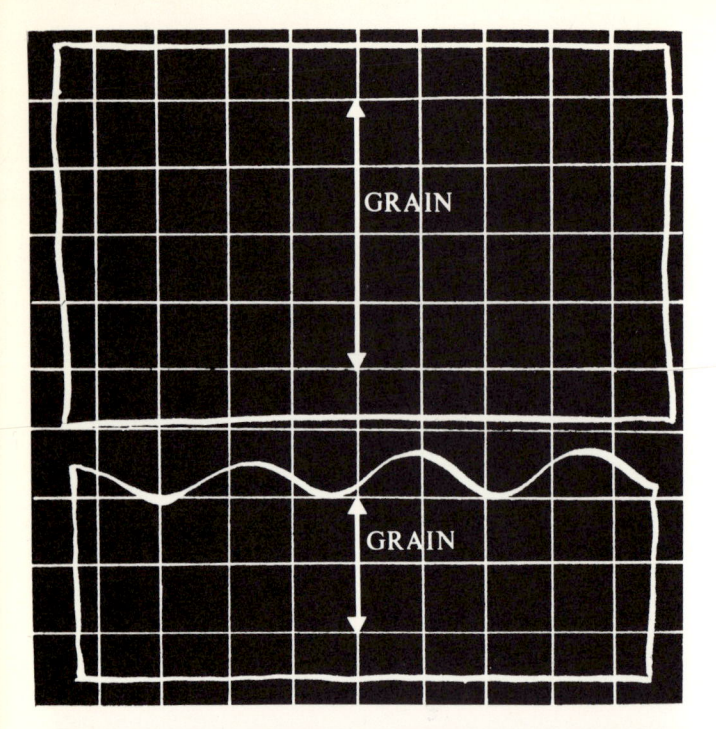

For each flower

Cut a strip of paper 152 mm (6 in.) wide and approximately 254 mm (10 in.) long, from one of the rolls of crêpe paper.

Cut a strip of paper from the other roll, 101 mm (4 in.) wide and 228 mm (9 in.) long. Cut one edge of this strip into a wavy line (see graph).

Bend one of the lengths of wire in half, twisting it round itself.

Fold the longest paper strip in half lengthways and roll it round the twisted wire, gluing the lower edge.

Wind the second strip onto the flower head, gluing it into position along the lower edge.

Stretch the upper edges of both strips so that they curl outwards.

Make sixteen flowers in this way and then twist all the stems together.

Bind the stem with a strip of crêpe paper.

Crêpe flower posy

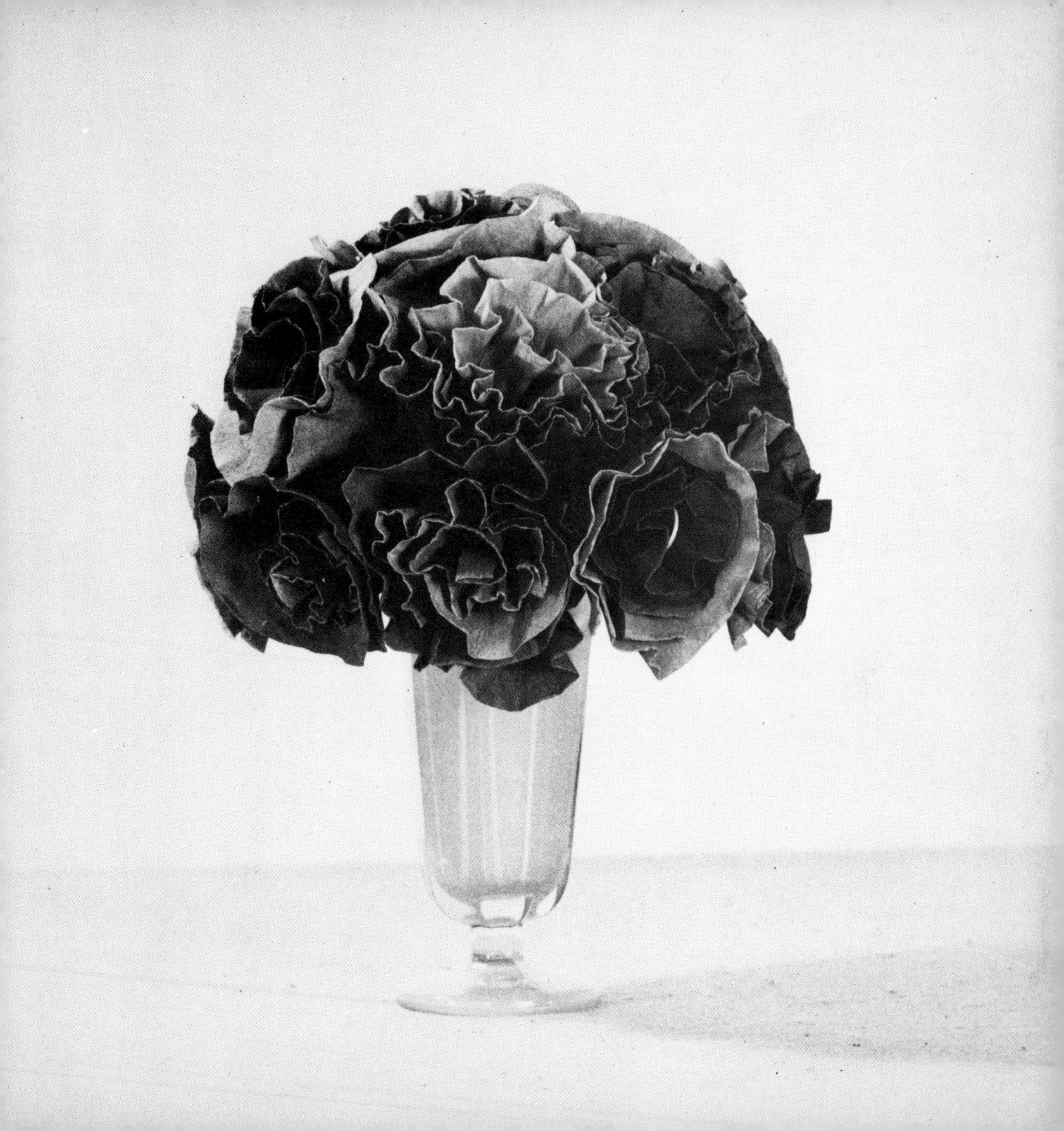

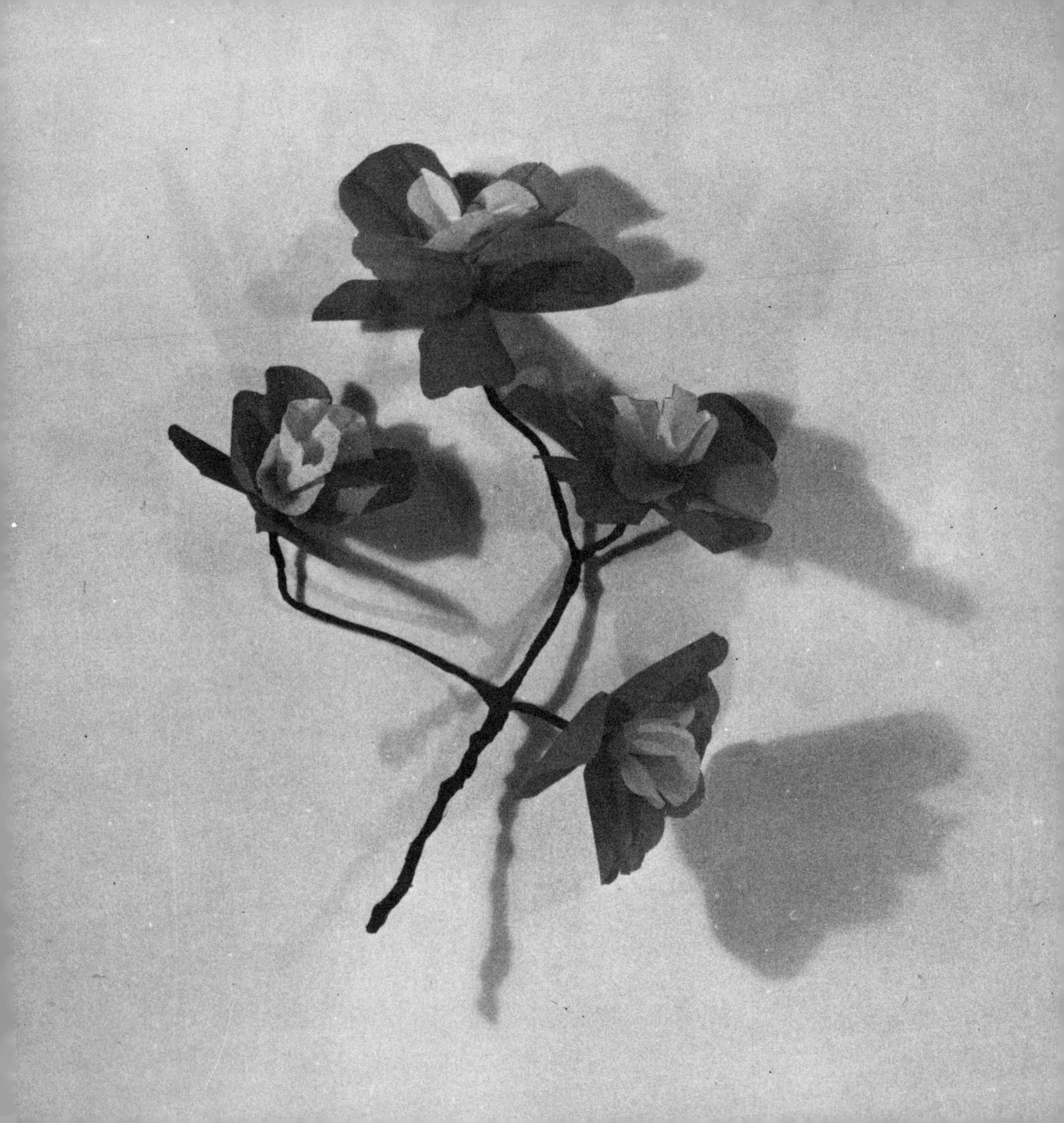

Crêpe flower branch

MATERIALS

Four lengths of medium weight wire, one 608 mm (24 in.), one 709 mm (28 in.), one 860 mm (34 in.) and one 406 mm (16 in.)
Three packets of crêpe paper in complementary colours
Strips of green crêpe paper
Scissors
Rubber solution glue
Pencil, graph paper 25 mm (1 in.) squares

Crêpe flower branch

METHOD

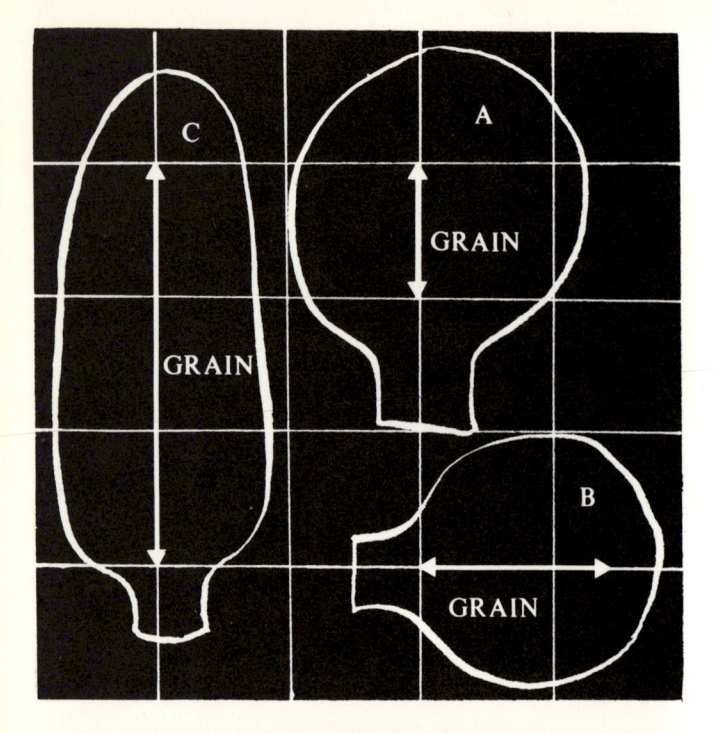

Make graph paper patterns from the graph [one square on the graph equals 25 mm (1 in.)].

For each flower, cut out four petals A, four petals B and four petals C, each set of petals being a different colour.

Bend each piece of wire in half, twisting it round itself.

Glue the petals onto the top of the stem, taking care to arrange each set of petals in a cross shape, with the set underneath showing in the spaces between the petals above.

Glue the petals on in this order, four As, four Bs, then four Cs.

The main stem is the longest. Twist the base of the other stems onto the main one, with the exception of the shortest stem, which is twisted onto one of the side stems.

Bind all the stems with strips of green crêpe paper glued into place.

TISSUE PAPER FLOWERS

INTRODUCTION

Tissue paper is sold in sheets measuring 508 mm (20 in.) by 762 mm (30 in.), generally in packets or rolls consisting of a single colour, or differing shades of a colour. There is a very pleasant range of colours, and the slight transparency of tissue leads to attractive colour combinations when different tones are mixed. The colours of tissue paper are rather prone to fading when they are subjected to direct sunlight and tissue paper flowers are therefore better placed in a shaded part of the room.
Because tissue paper is so thin, any bulkiness needed in a flower is obtained by using many layers, this gives a softness and delicacy of outline to the finished flower. If the tissue paper used has been bought in a packet, iron out the creases before making flowers from it.

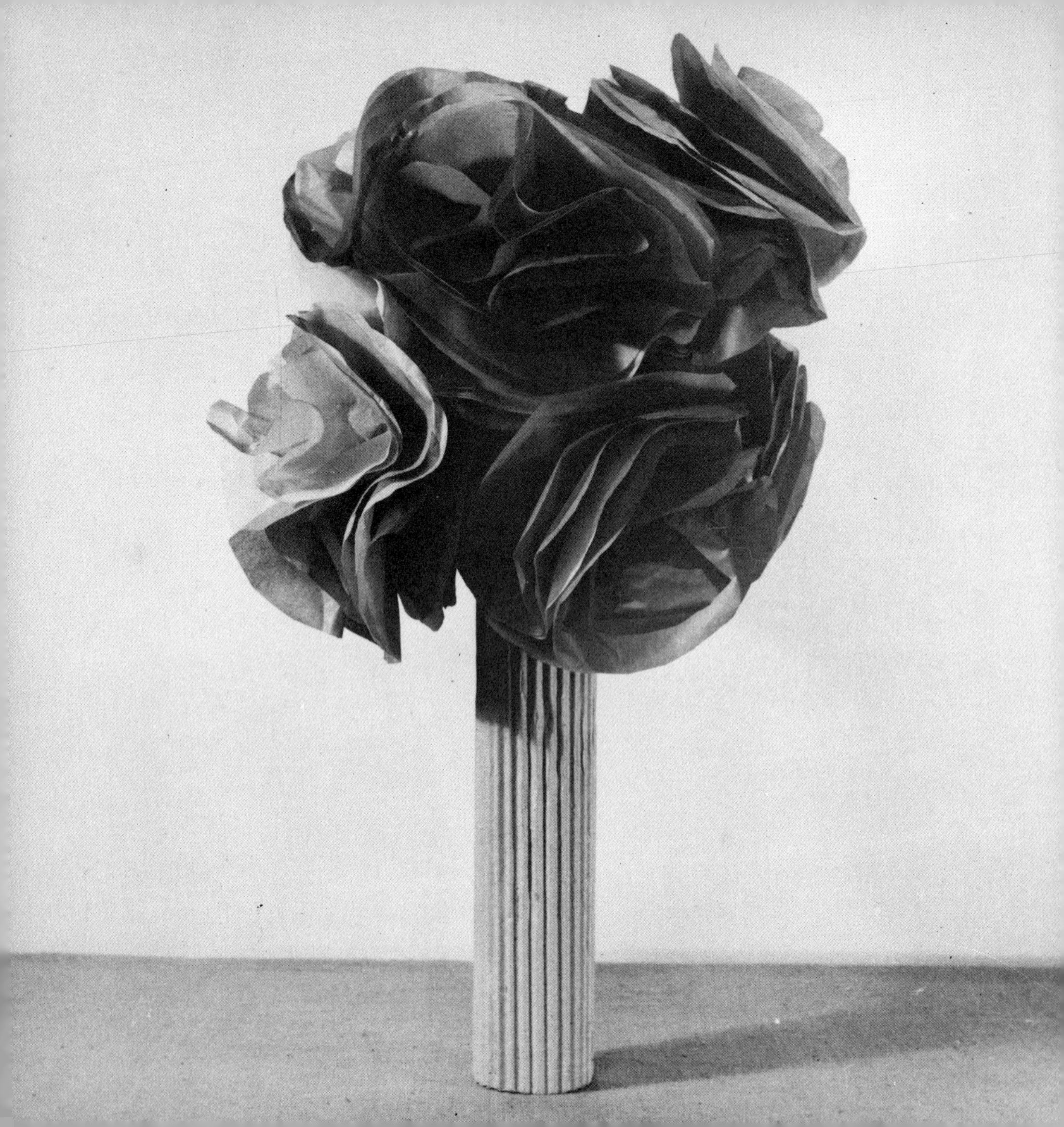

Simple tissue flower

MATERIALS

A piece of thick wire 431 mm (17 in.) long, or a split bamboo stick of the same length
Five sheets of tissue paper (this makes three flowers)
Choose three vivid colours that blend well
Rubber solution glue
Scissors
A dinner plate, approximately 228 mm (9 in.) in diameter
Pencil, tracing paper

Simple tissue flower

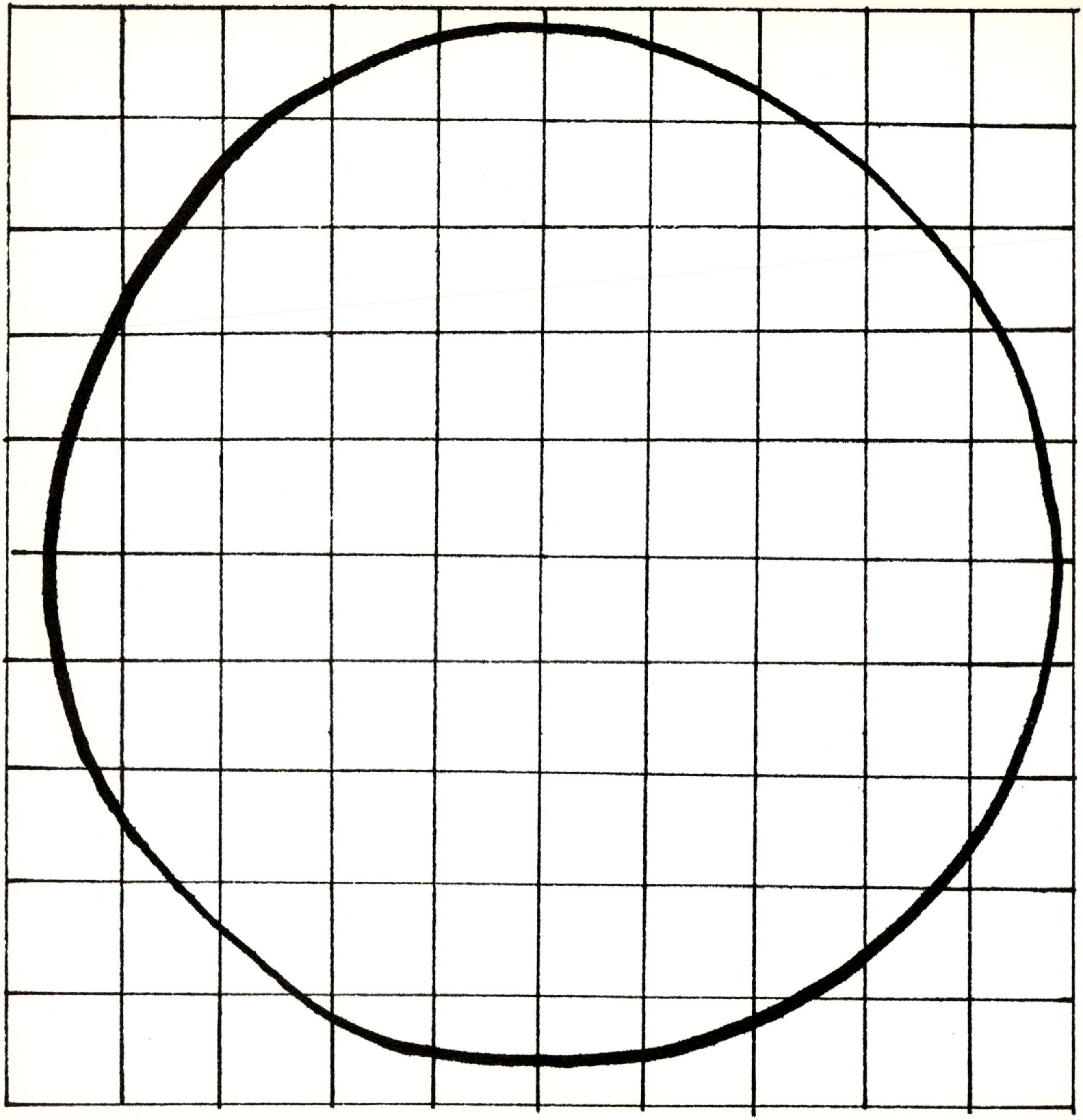

METHOD

Fold the five sheets of tissue into sixths and lay the dinner plate onto the folded paper. Draw round the edge of the plate. If no plate is available, make a tracing direct from the graph on the facing page and transfer it to the tissue.
Cut out the paper on the pencil line.
Dab glue onto the tip of the wire stem and pierce the centre of one of the tissue paper circles with the glued end of the stem.
Holding the centre of the tissue paper circle between the finger tips of one hand and the tip of the wire in the other, twist the wire and the tissue gently in opposite directions so that the tissue gathers up slightly round the stem. Add further circles, alternating the colours and twisting each time. When ten circles have been added, put a tiny dab of glue onto the innermost circle and press the opposite side of this circle onto the glue so that the tip of the wire is hidden.

(Overleaf) Tissue flower quatrefoil

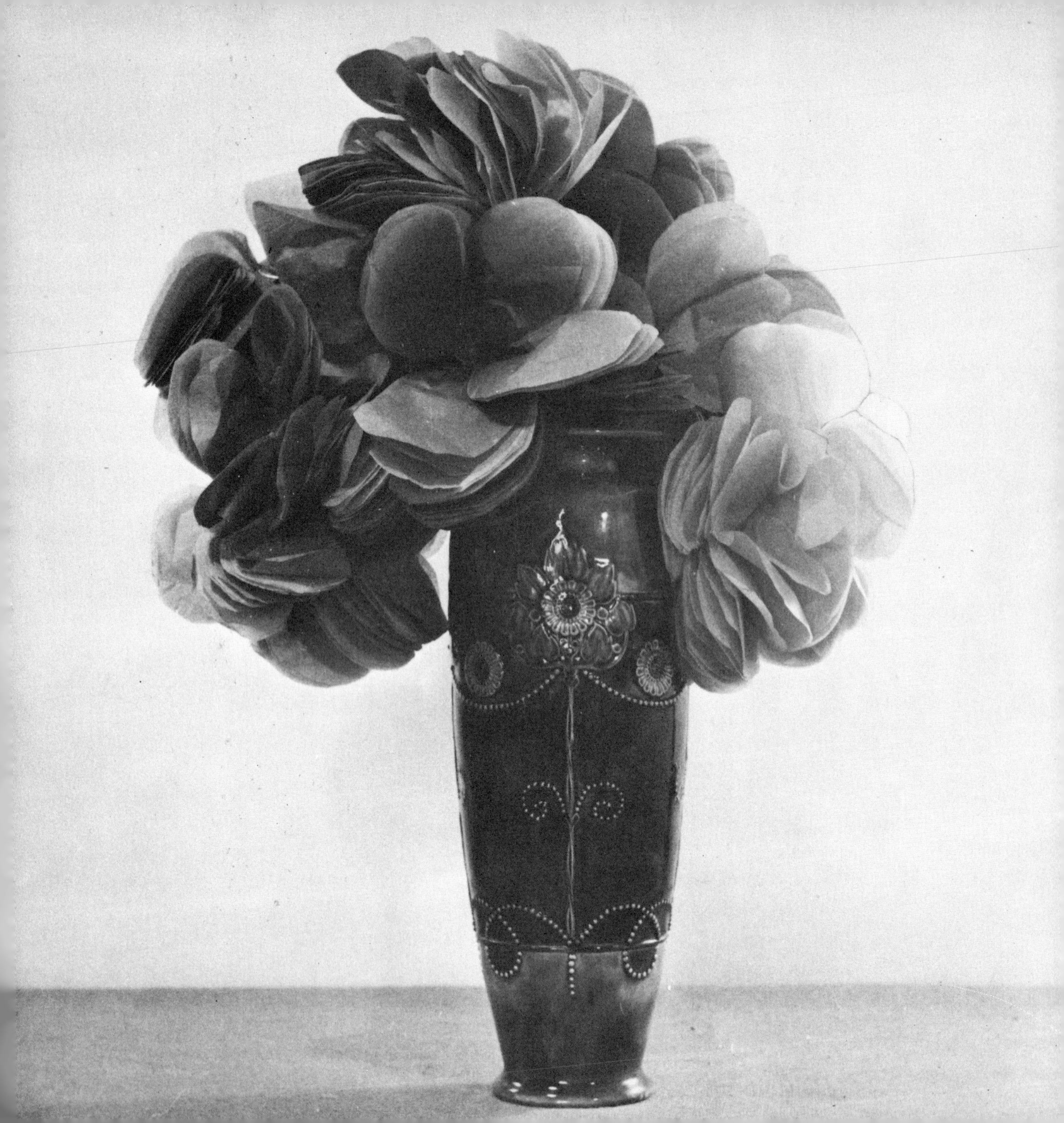

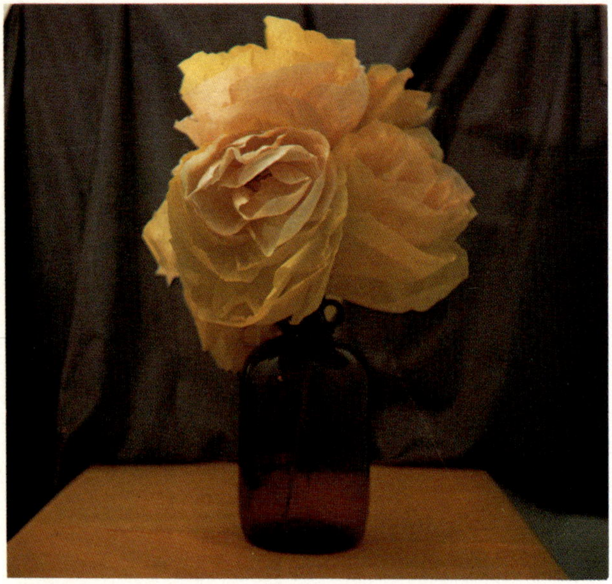
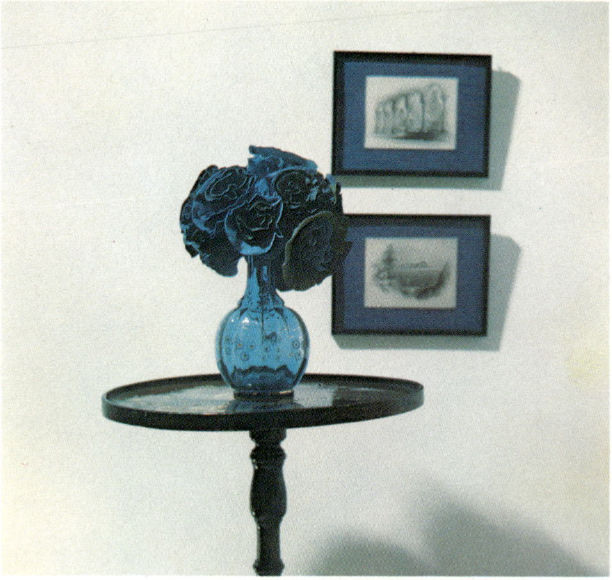
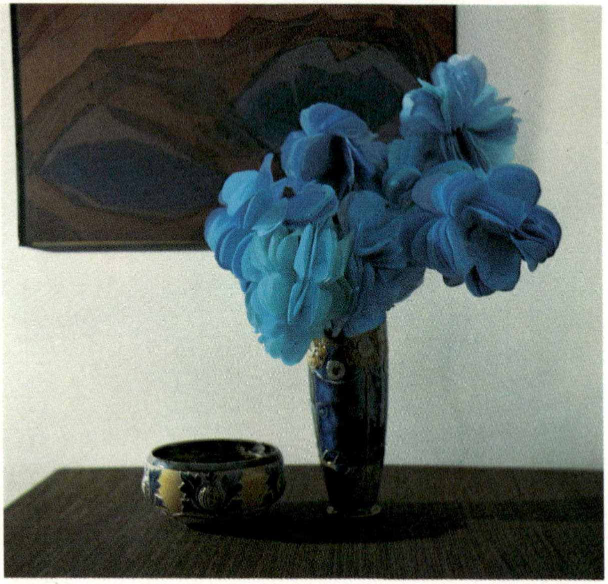
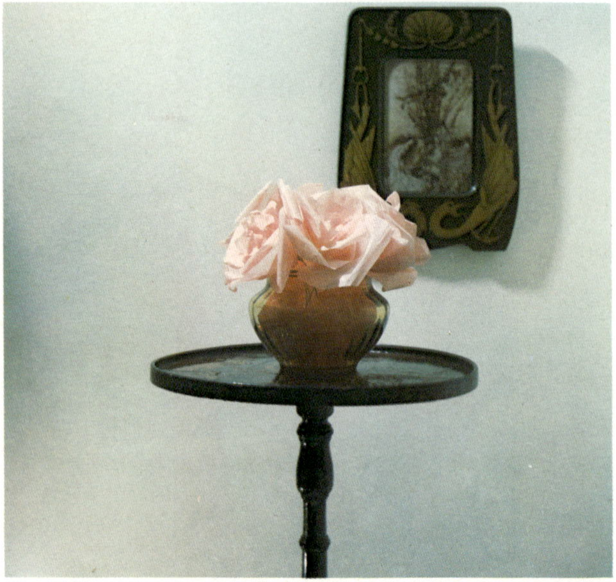

Tissue flower quatrefoil

MATERIALS

A piece of medium weight wire 558 mm (22 in.) long,
or a split bamboo stick of the same length
One sheet of dark blue tissue paper
One sheet of pale blue tissue paper
Scissors
Pencil, graph paper 25 mm (1 in.) squares

PLATE 2a *(Opposite above left)* Simple crêpe
flower with shaped petals
2b *(Opposite above right)* Crêpe flower posy
2c *(Opposite below left)* Tissue flower quatrefoil
2d *(Opposite below right)* Tissue paper rose

METHOD

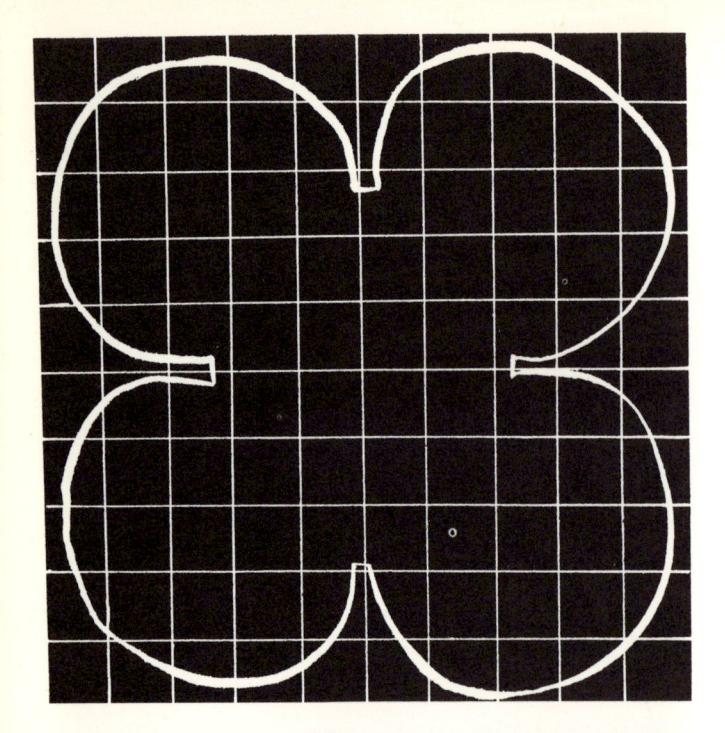

Make a pattern from the graph above [one square on the graph being equal to 25 mm (1 in.)].
Fold the sheets of tissue into sixths and lay the cut out graph paper pattern onto the folded tissue.
Draw round the pattern and cut out the shape along the pencil line.
Make the flowers up as for the first tissue paper flower, page 47.

Tissue paper cabbage rose

MATERIALS

Four sheets tissue paper, dark blue
Four sheets tissue paper, mid blue
Four sheets tissue paper, pale blue
A length of thick wire, 431 mm (17 in.), or a split bamboo stick of the same length.
Rubber solution glue
Scissors
Pencil, graph paper 25 mm (1 in.) squares

METHOD

Make a graph paper pattern from the graph [one square on the graph equals 25 mm (1 in.)] and cut it out.

Fold the sheets of tissue into eighths and lay the graph paper pattern onto the folded paper.

Draw round the pattern and cut out the shape along the pencil line.

Hold all the layers together between the first finger and thumb of each hand at points A and B, and push inwards so that the central 'bridge' of paper folds up. Bend one end of the wire stem round the 'bridge' and then bend the wire round itself down the length of the stem.

Hold the flower head downwards and shake it sharply to separate the layers.

Working from the lowest petals on each side, interleave them at C and D.

Tissue paper cabbage rose

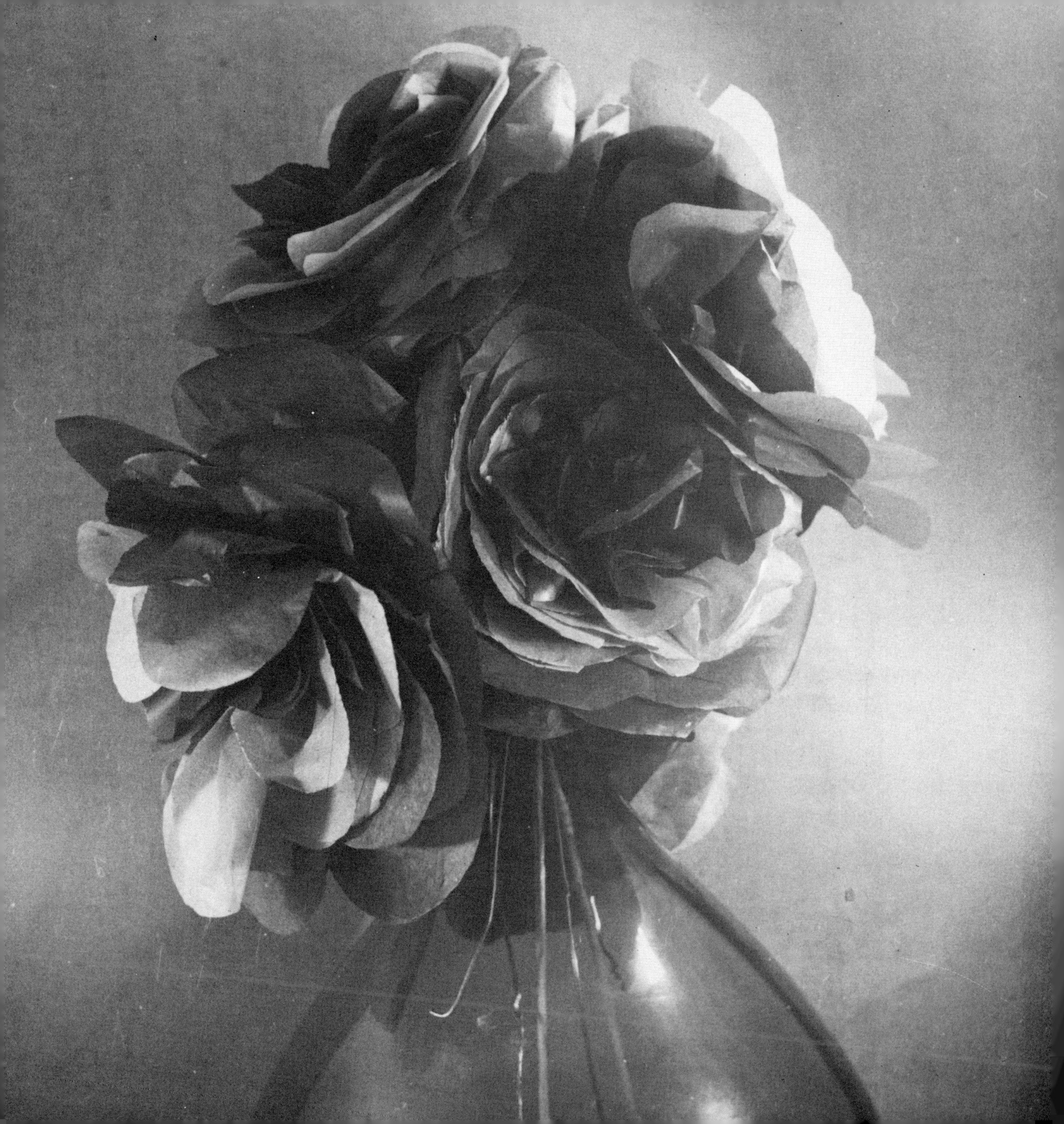

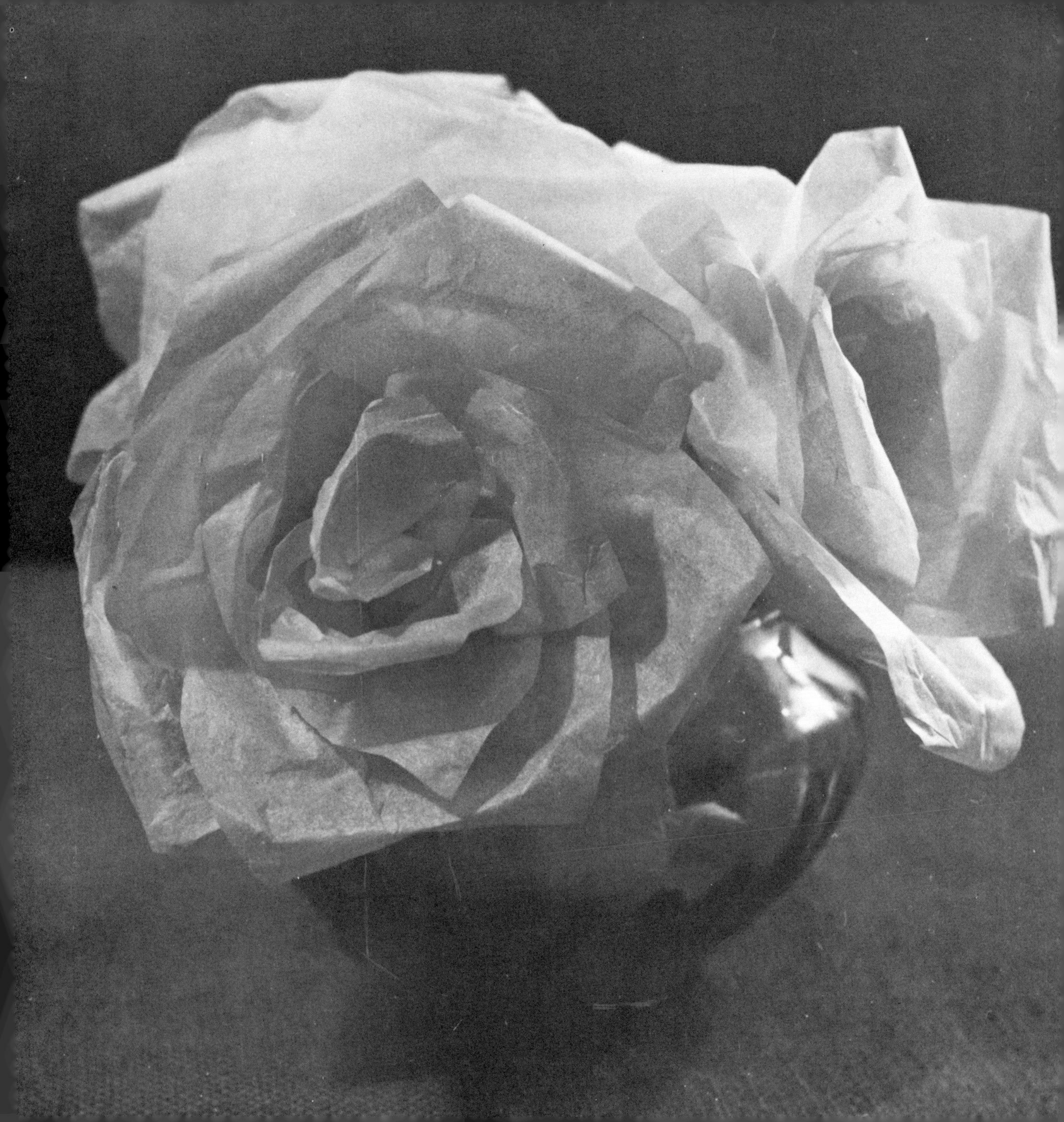

Tissue paper rose

MATERIALS

A piece of medium weight wire 304 mm (12 in.) long,
or a split bamboo stick of the same length
One sheet of pink tissue paper
Rubber solution glue
A knitting needle
Scissors
Pencil, graph paper 25 mm (1 in.) squares

Tissue paper rose

METHOD

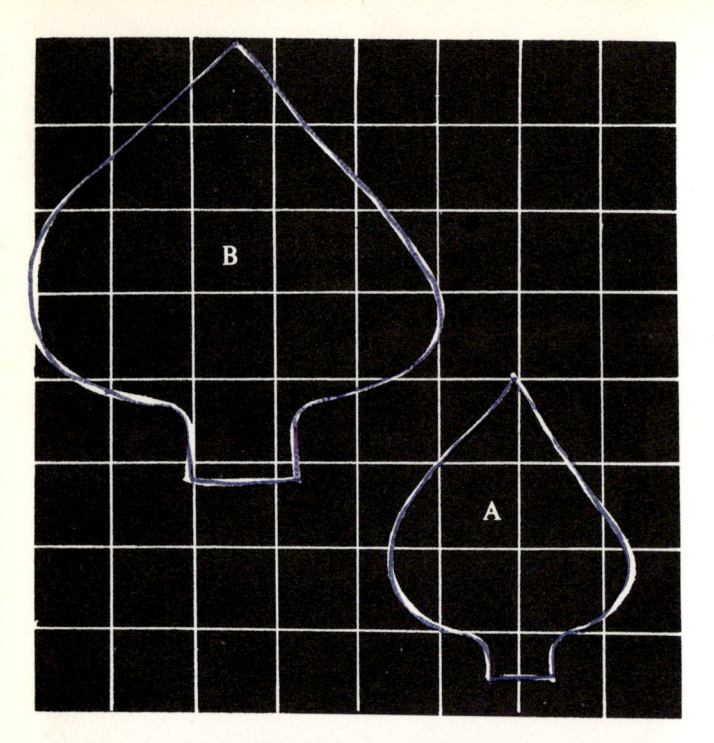

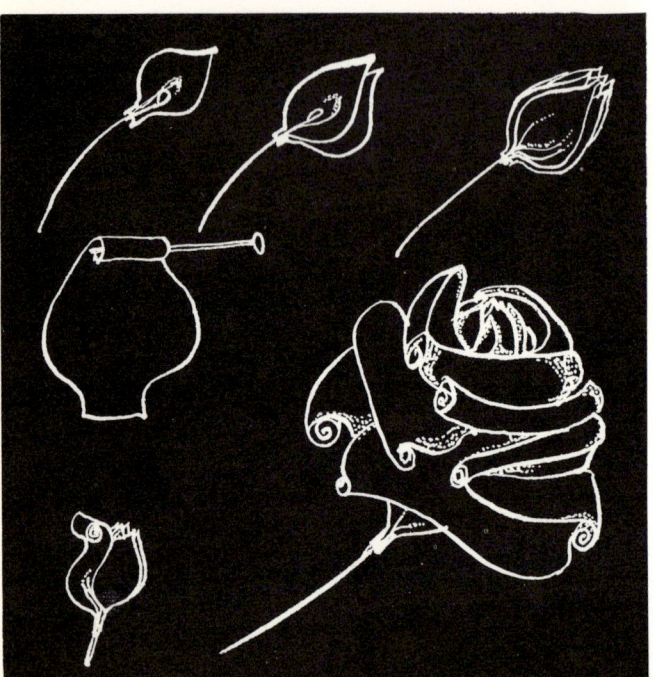

Make graph paper patterns for both the shapes shown on the graph [one square on the graph equals 25 mm (1 in.)] and cut them out.
Fold the tissue paper into eighths, lay both patterns onto the folded paper and draw round them.
Cut out the shapes along the pencil lines.
Glue the eight petals A round the tip of the wire stem, gathering the bases of the petals slightly and overlapping the edges.
Roll the tip of each petal B round the knitting needle so that they curl over.
Glue the petals B round the centre of the flower, gathering the bases slightly and overlapping the edges of the petals.
These roses can be made in the same way from silver cooking foil; handle the foil very gently as it is inclined to crush and tear.

Tissue flower ball

MATERIALS

Four sheets of tissue paper, crimson, magenta, pink and orange
Thirty six hairpins
Styrofoam ball for dry flower arrangements
1·8 m (2 yards) of pink satin ribbon, 12 mm ($\frac{1}{2}$ in.) wide
Rubber solution glue
Pencil, tracing paper

(Overleaf) Tissue flower ball

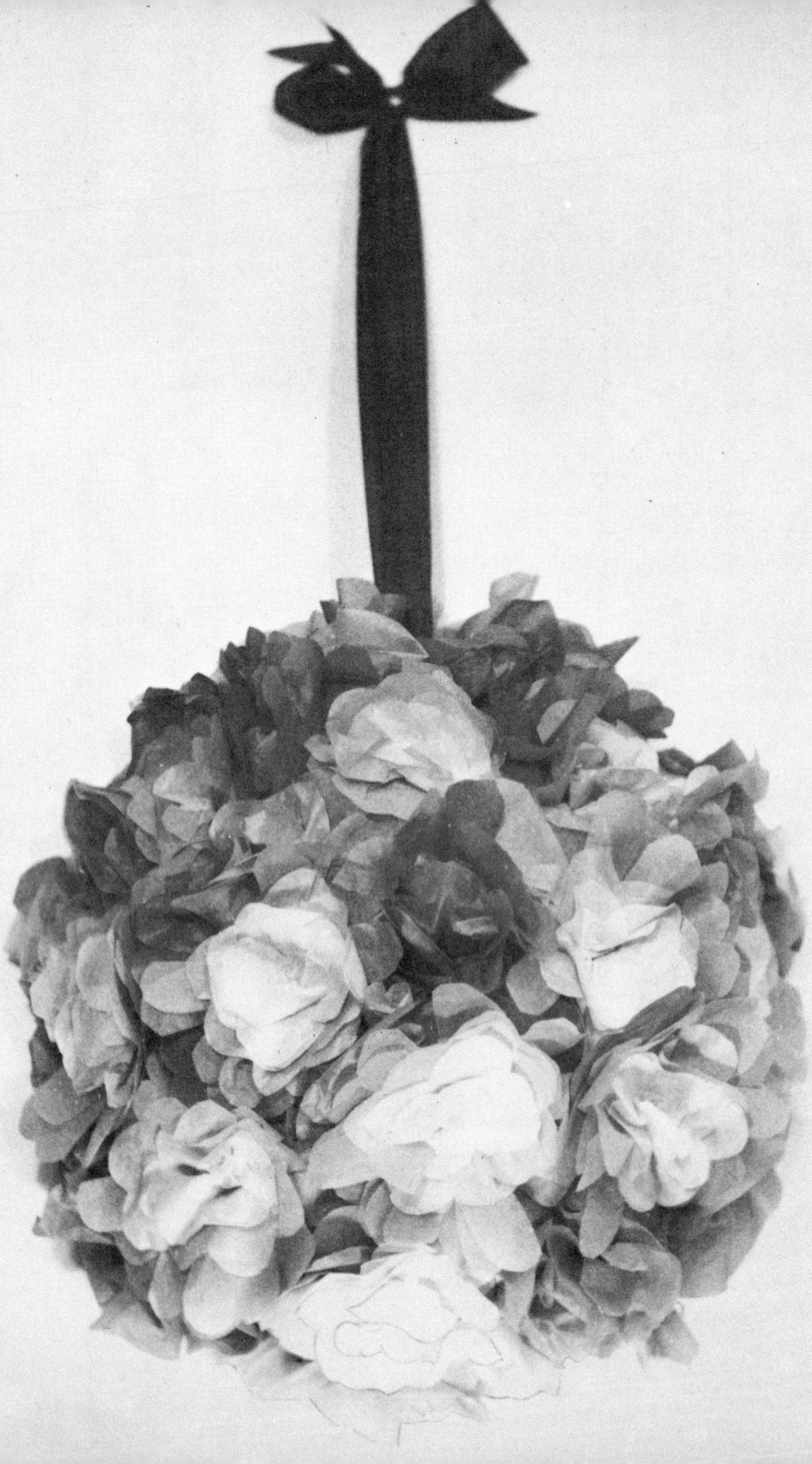

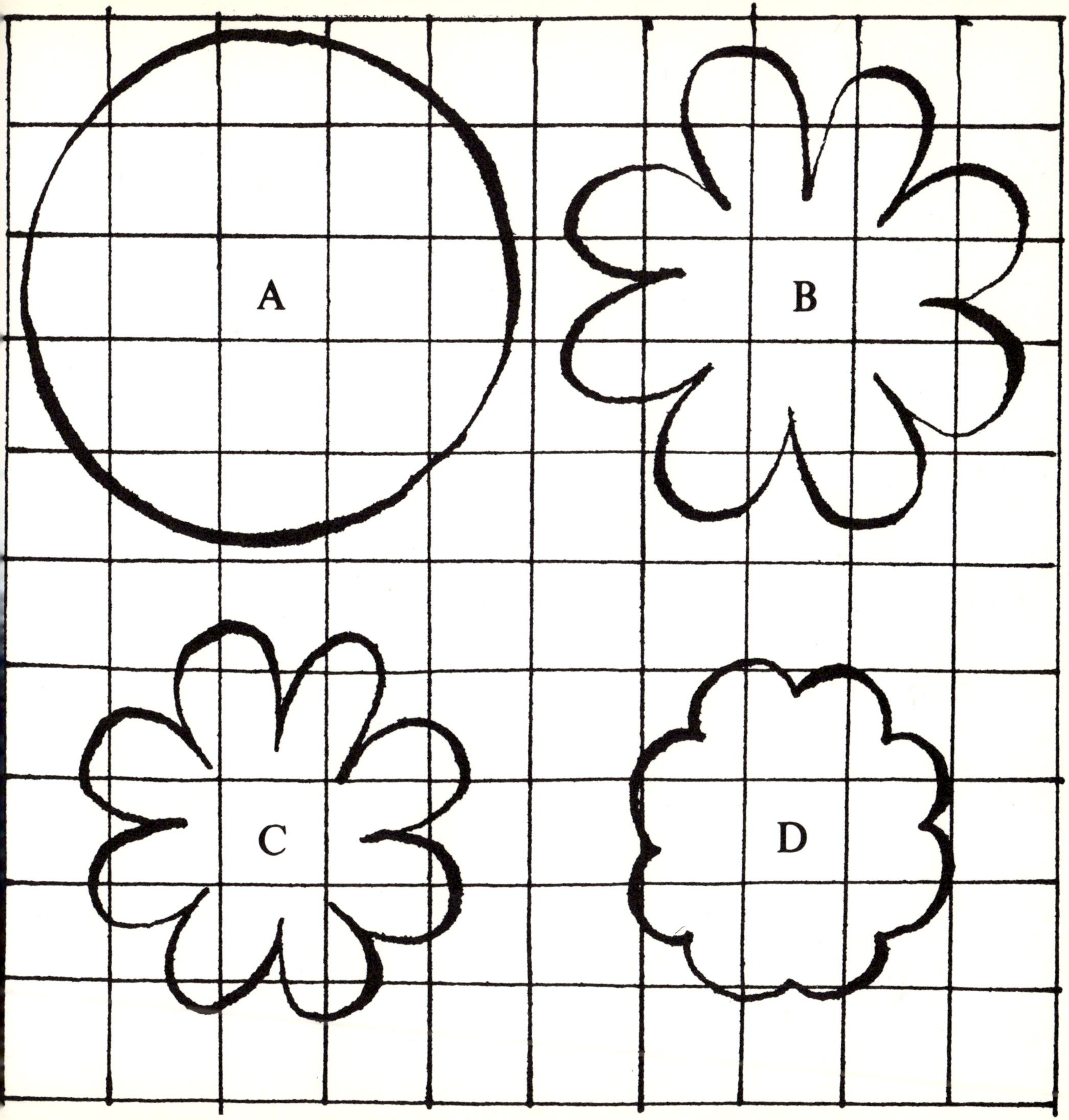
A
B
C
D

METHOD

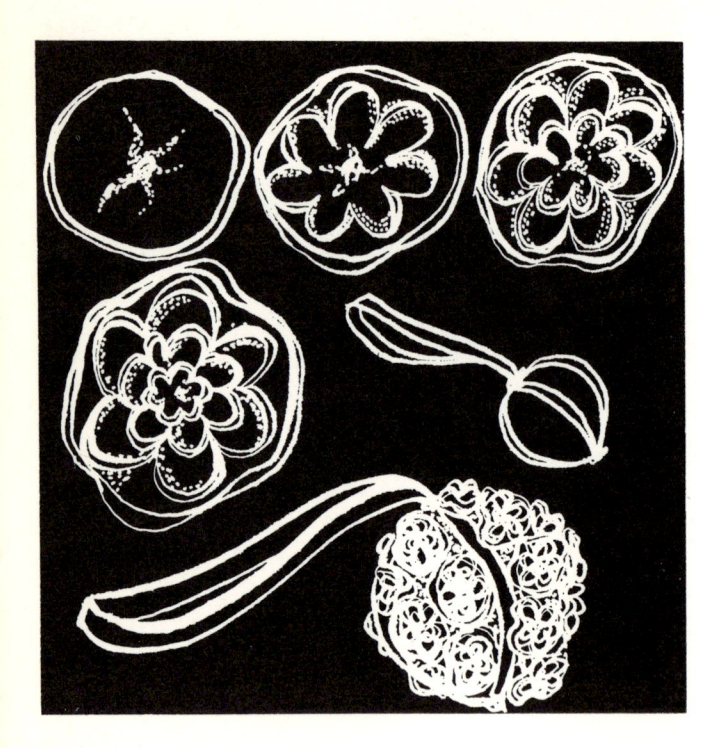

Trace a pattern for each of the shapes on the graph shown on the previous page. Cut out each shape.
Lay the cut out shapes onto the folded sheets of tissue paper and cut seventy two pieces from each pattern piece. The colours can be used in a random way, or restricted to each shape. Each little flower consists of two layers of each of the four shapes.

For each flower

Take one shape A and put a little dab of glue in the centre of it. Lay another shape A on top of the first and pierce both in the centre with the points of a hairpin. The bent end of the hairpin should protrude about 7 mm ($\frac{1}{4}$ in.) above the centre of the tissue.
Place another dab of glue on the protruding tip of the hairpin and stick one shape B onto it. Pinch the centre of the shape slightly so that the edges of it lift away from the A shapes beneath.
Add another dab of glue to the centre of the tissue and place the second shape B in position. Again pinch it slightly round the bent tip of the hairpin. Add the two shapes C and the two shapes D in the same way.
Make thirty six flowers.
Tie the satin ribbon round the florist's ball so that it is firmly held and the ribbon forms a loop.
Drive the points of the hairpins into the ball, so that when pushed in, the little flowers lie closely packed all over the surface.

Tissue flower cone

MATERIALS

Ten sheets of tissue paper, two sheets each of pink, red, orange, yellow and brown
One sheet of white card, 508 mm (20 in.) by 608 mm (24 in.)
Four plain postcards 152 mm × 76 mm (6 in. × 3 in.)
Rubber solution glue
Scissors
Pencil, graph paper, black felt tip pen

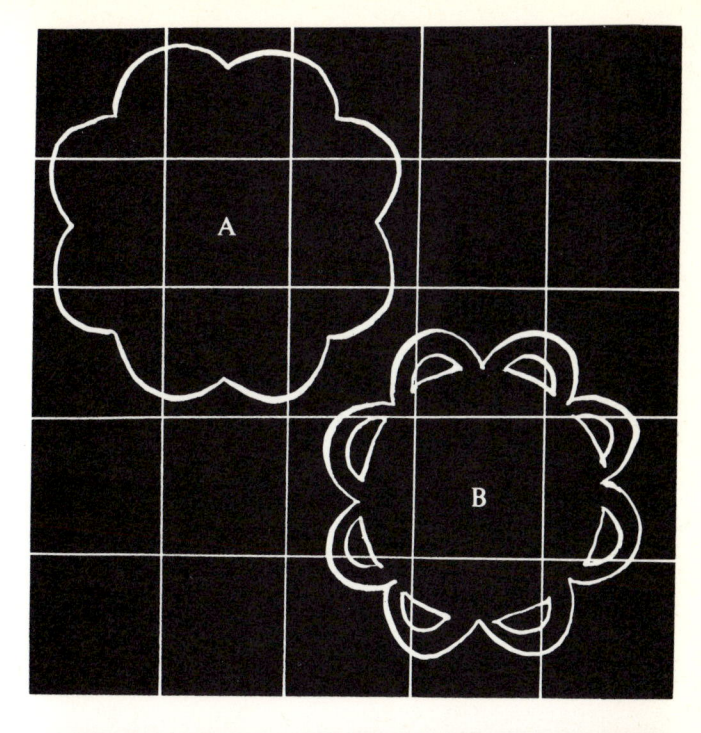

METHOD

Make a graph paper pattern for each of the shapes given on the graphs shown on the previous page. Cut out the pattern shapes.
Lay the shapes on the folded tissue paper and cut out seventy two shapes of each from the tissue paper.
Mark all the shapes with the felt pen in the patterns shown on the graphs.
Cut the postcards into 25 mm (1 in.) squares.

For each flower

Dab glue in the centre of each postcard square and place one shape A on it, pinching the centre slightly. Add all the other pieces in the order B, C, D, pinching the centre of each one. Make seventy two little flowers like this.
Bend the corners of the large sheet of card round so it forms a cone.
Glue the cone into position firmly and trim the base so that it will stand.
Put a dab of glue onto the card at the back of each little flower. Stick the flowers onto the cone.

Tissue flower cone

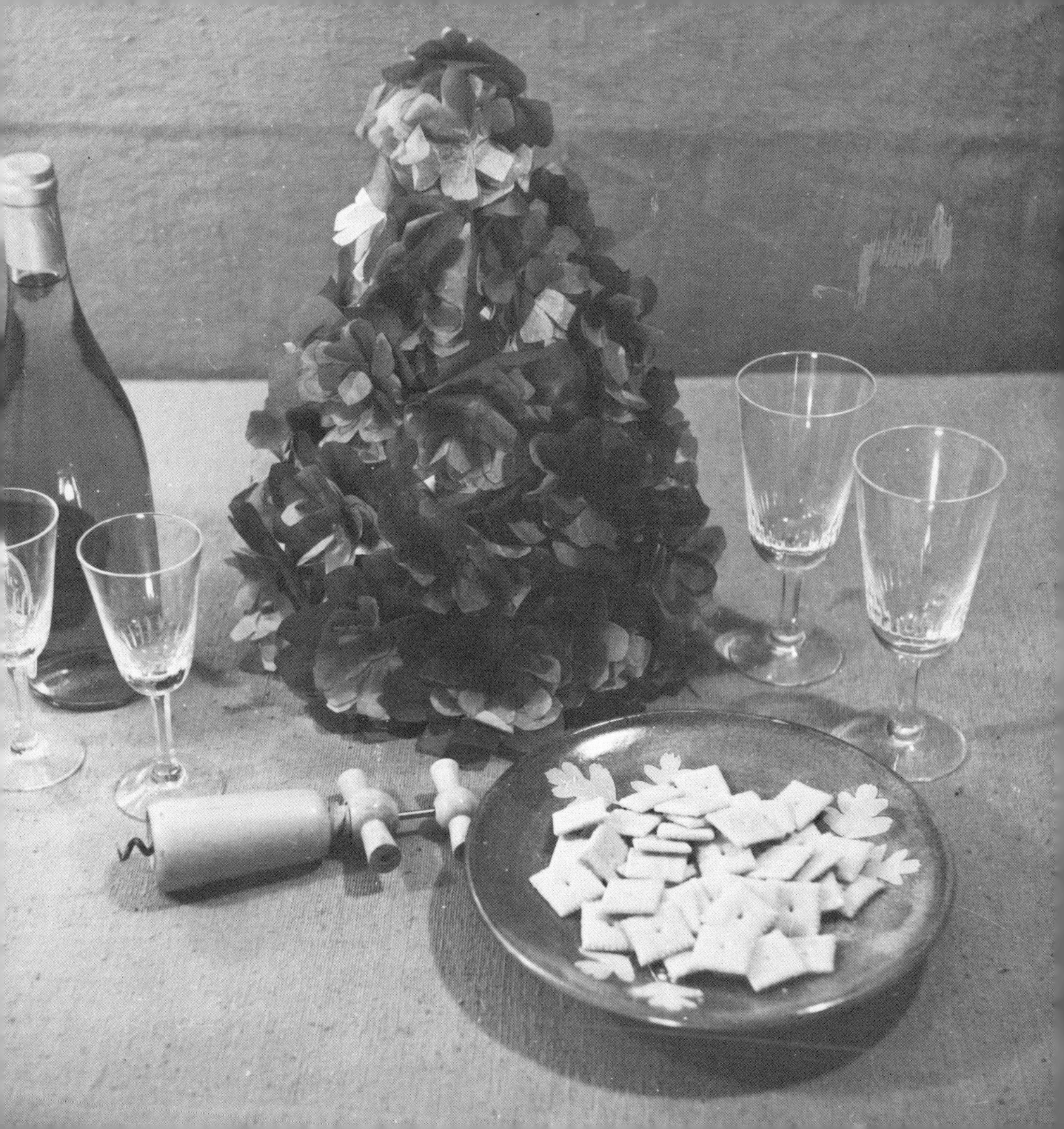

CARTRIDGE PAPER FLOWERS

INTRODUCTION

Cartridge paper is sold in varying sizes, from sheets the size of writing paper to rolls at least 762 mm (30 in.) wide and sold by the yard. The most suitable size is a sheet about 762 mm × 558 mm (30 in. × 22 in.) about 75 gsm (a 45 lb weight), ie the weight of a ream of this paper.
The instructions in this section all apply to a sheet of paper in this size and weight.
Cartridge paper is usually a white or creamy colour, but it is obtainable in a variety of tints and it can be painted. If this is done, it is better to paint the cartridge paper before the flower is made up from it, rather than paint the finished flower. Small areas of colour can be added after the flower is made, but to paint the whole flower would tend to make it limp and shapeless. Cartridge paper has a crispness that lends a sculptural quality to the flowers and the paper can be scored and bent into shape.

PLATE 3a *(Opposite above left)* Crêpe flower with padded centre
3b *(Opposite above right)* Cartridge paper buttercup
3c *(Opposite below left)* Cartridge paper daisy
3d *(Opposite below right)* Dish arrangement

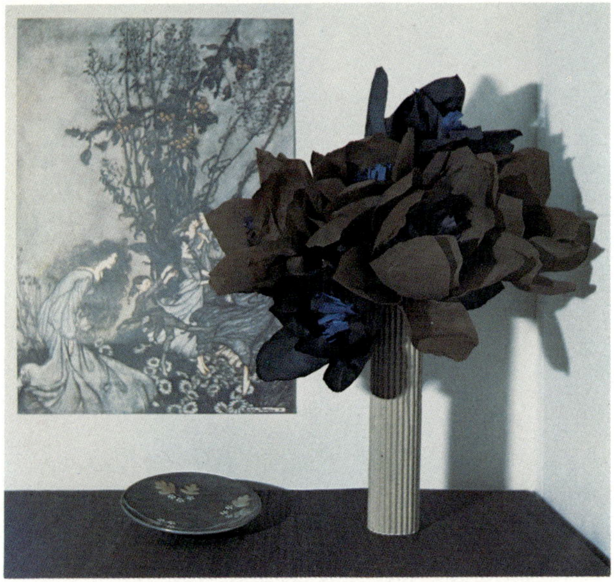
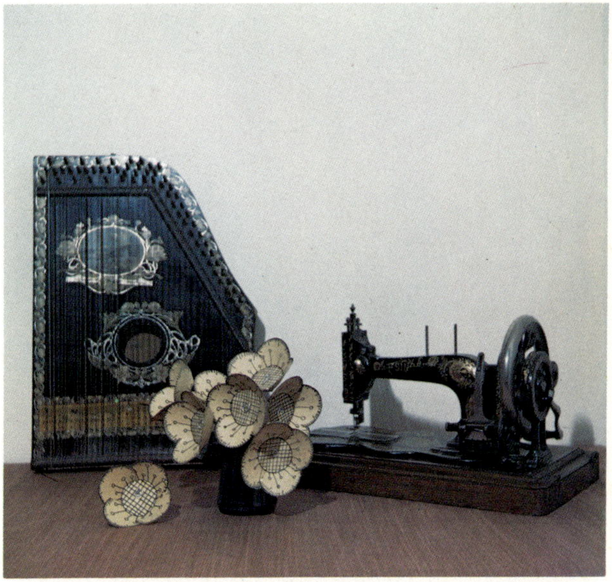
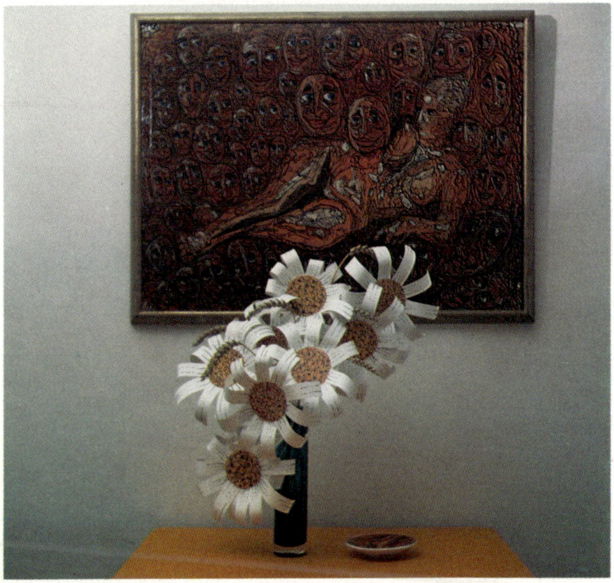
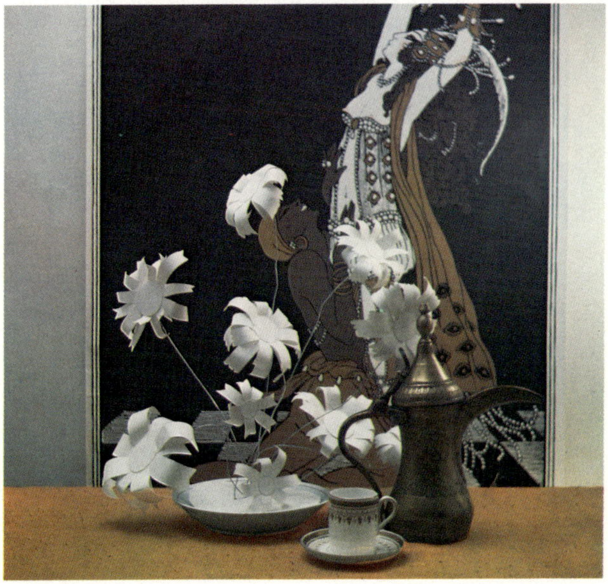

Cartridge paper buttercup

MATERIALS

One sheet of yellow cartridge paper (or paint white paper yellow on both sides)
Fifteen lengths of medium weight wire, each 203 mm (8 in.) long
A strip of green crêpe paper (optional)
Rubber solution glue or a stapler
Scissors
Wax candle
Pencil, tracing paper, black felt pen

(Overleaf) Cartridge paper buttercup

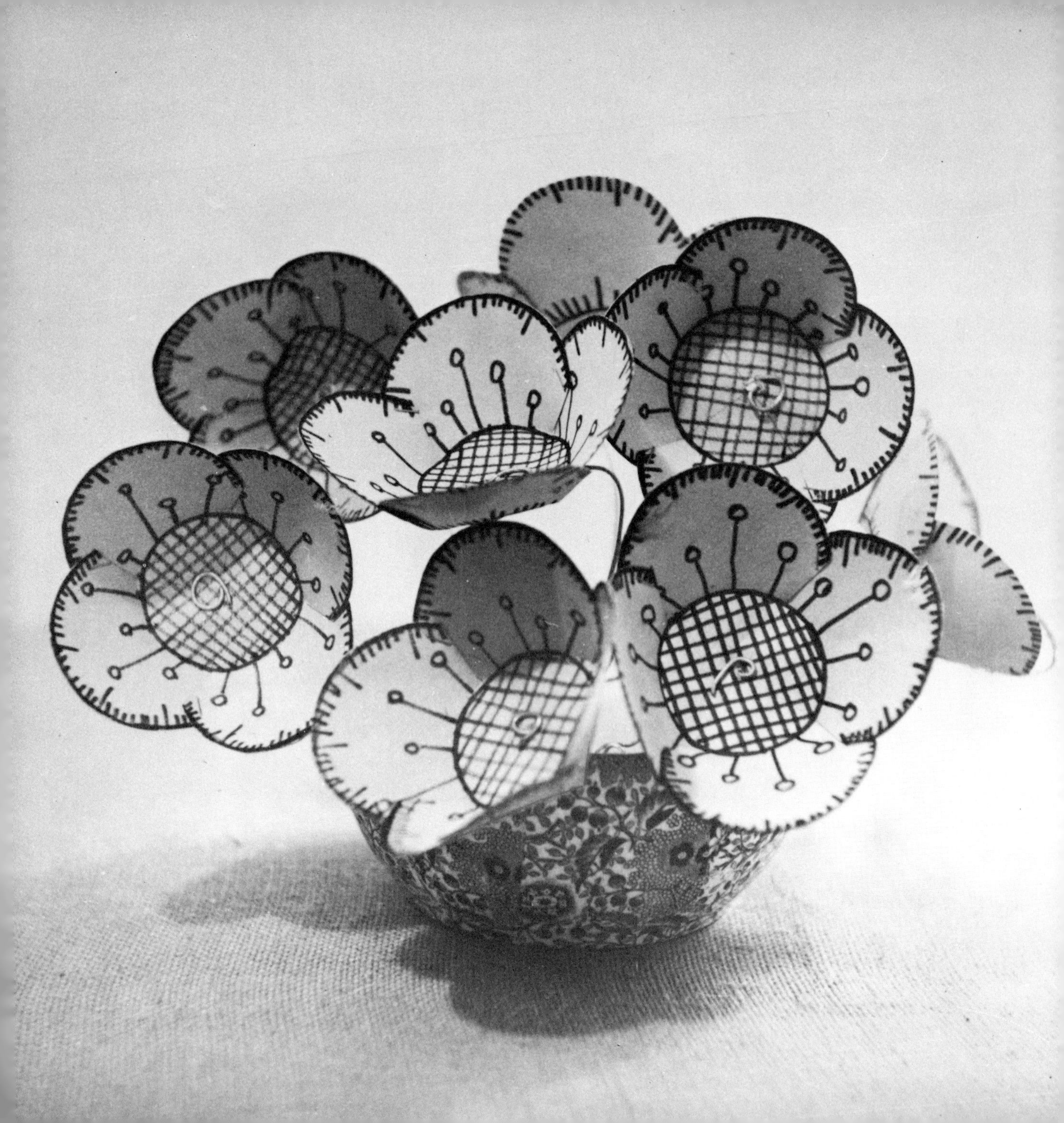

A

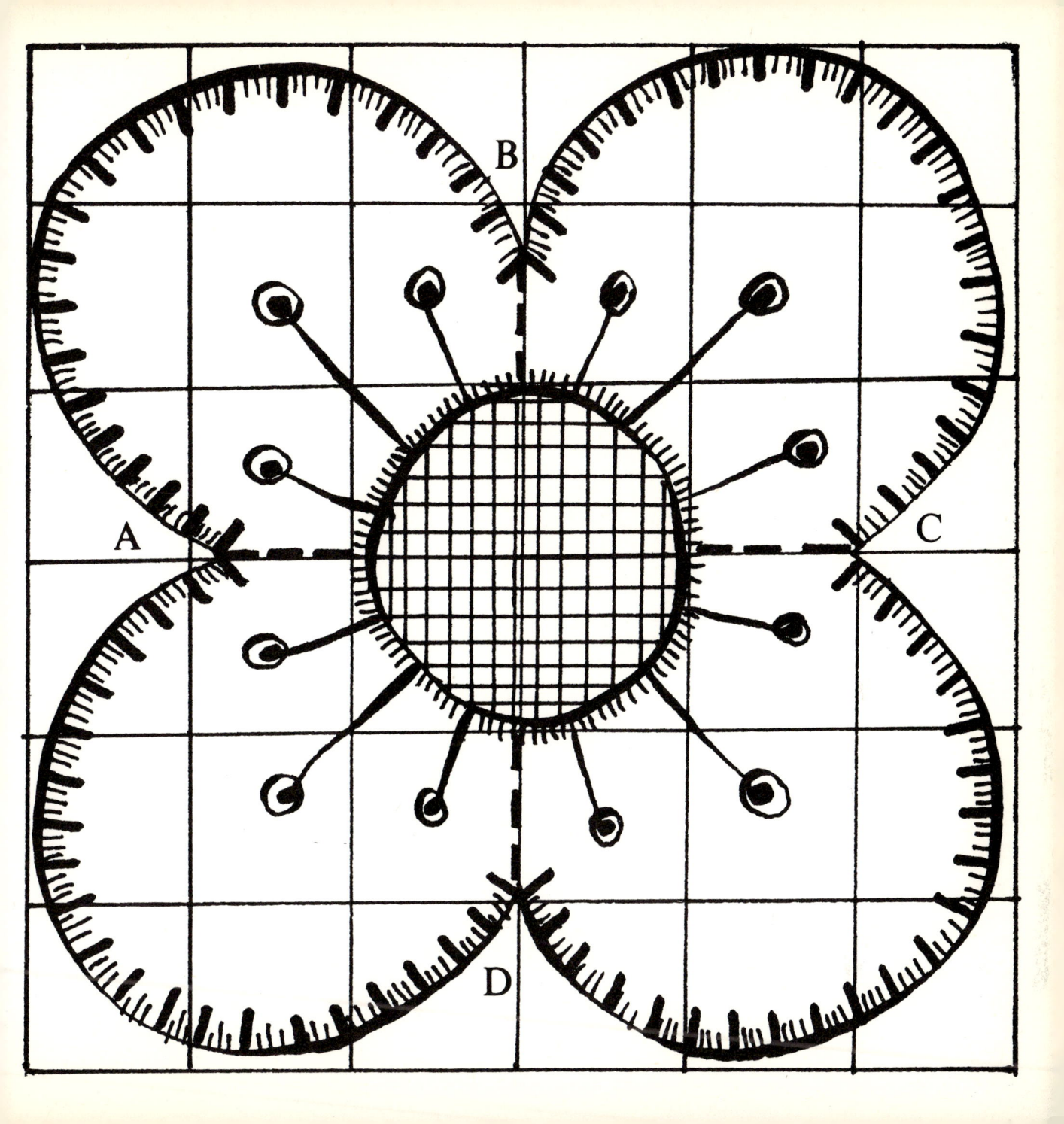

B

C

D

METHOD

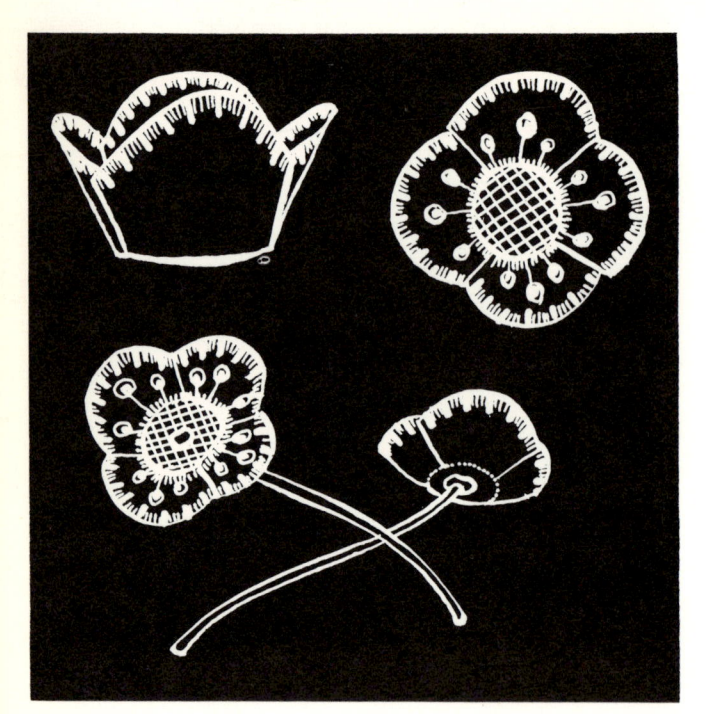

Make a tracing paper pattern from the graph on the previous page.

Cut out the pattern and use it as a template to make fifteen flowers.

Using the felt pen, draw in the markings shown on the graph on each flower head.

Snip into the flowers at A, B, C and D. Each snip should be 25 mm (1 in.) long.

Overlap the edges of each snip and glue or staple them, this will cause the petals to stand up and form the cup.

Push the end of the wire through the centre of the flower.

Light the candle and allow a drop of melted wax to fall on the tip of the wire inside the flower. This will hold the wire steady.

Bind the stems with strips of green crêpe paper if you wish.

Cartridge paper daisy

MATERIALS

A piece of thick wire 254 mm (10 in.) long
One sheet of white cartridge paper
Orange paint
Rubber solution glue
Scissors
A cork
Pencil, tracing paper, black felt tip pen

(Overleaf) Cartridge paper daisy

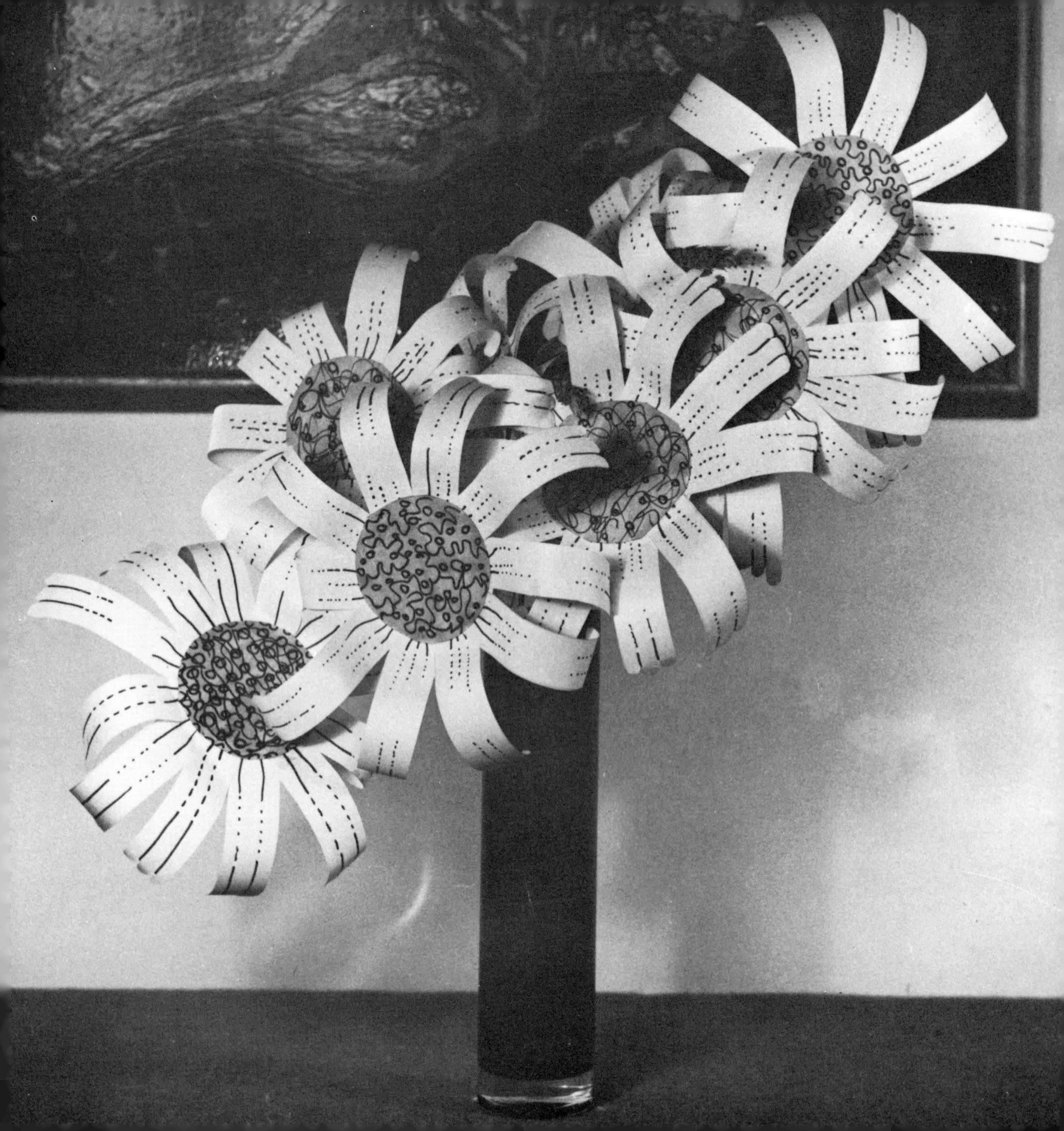

B

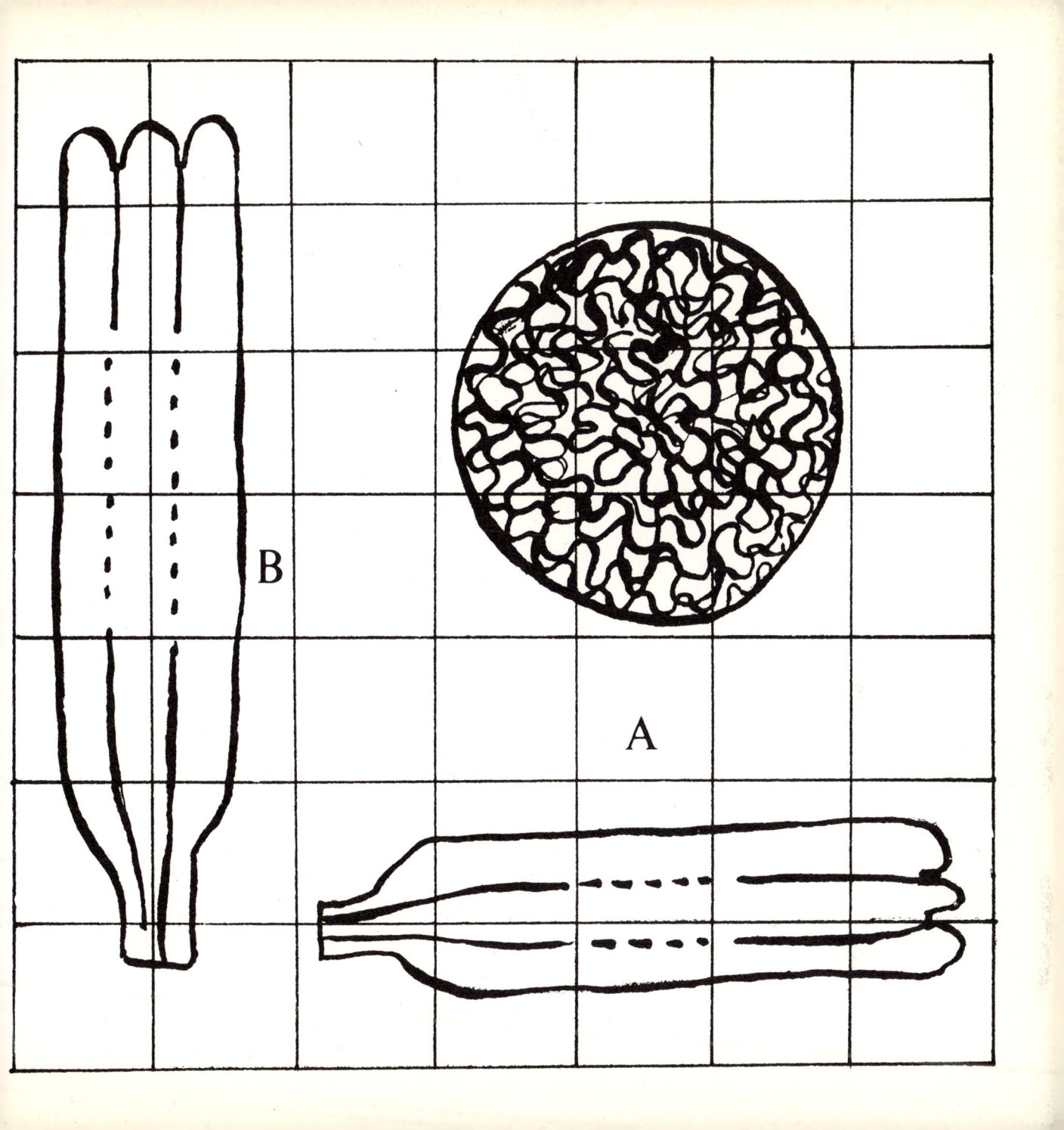

A

METHOD

Make tracing paper patterns from the graph on the previous page.
Cut out the patterns and use them as templates. Cut out twelve petals A and twelve petals B from the white cartridge paper.
Cut out two circles and paint one of them orange.
Decorate all the petals and the orange circle with the black felt pen, as shown on the graph.
Stick the twelve petals A to the back of the decorated circle and then the twelve petals B.
Stick the plain circle to the back of the decorated circle.
Curl the petals by pulling them gently between the thumb and the blunt side of the scissors.
Cut the cork in half and glue one half to the centre back of the flower and drive the tip of the wire stem into the cork.

Cartridge paper tulip

MATERIALS

A piece of thick wire 254 mm (10 in.) long, or a split bamboo stick of the same length
One sheet of red cartridge paper (or paint white paper red on both sides)
Masking tape
Scissors
A strip of green crêpe paper
Pencil, tracing paper, black felt tip pen
Red ink

(Overleaf) Cartridge paper tulip

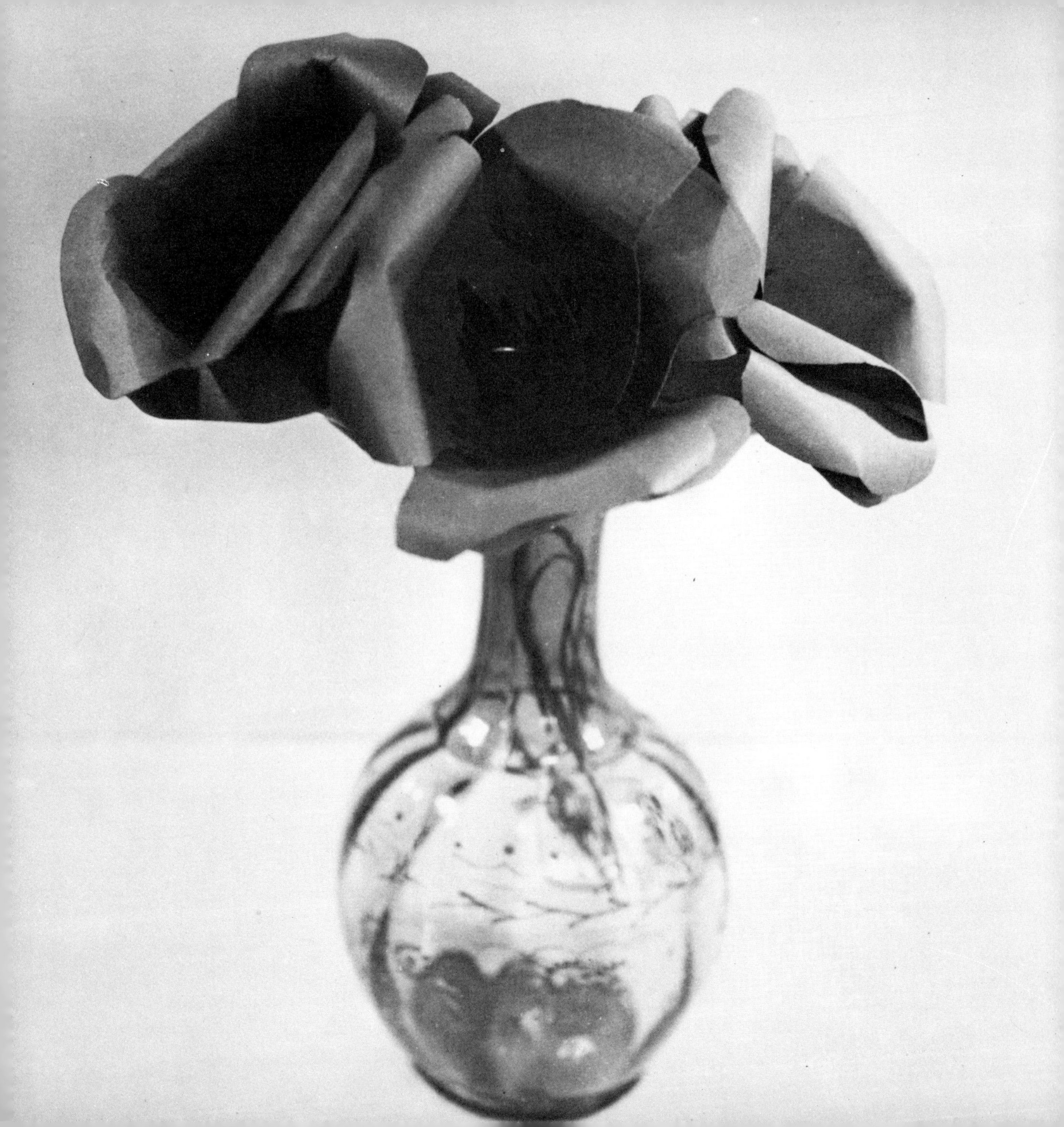

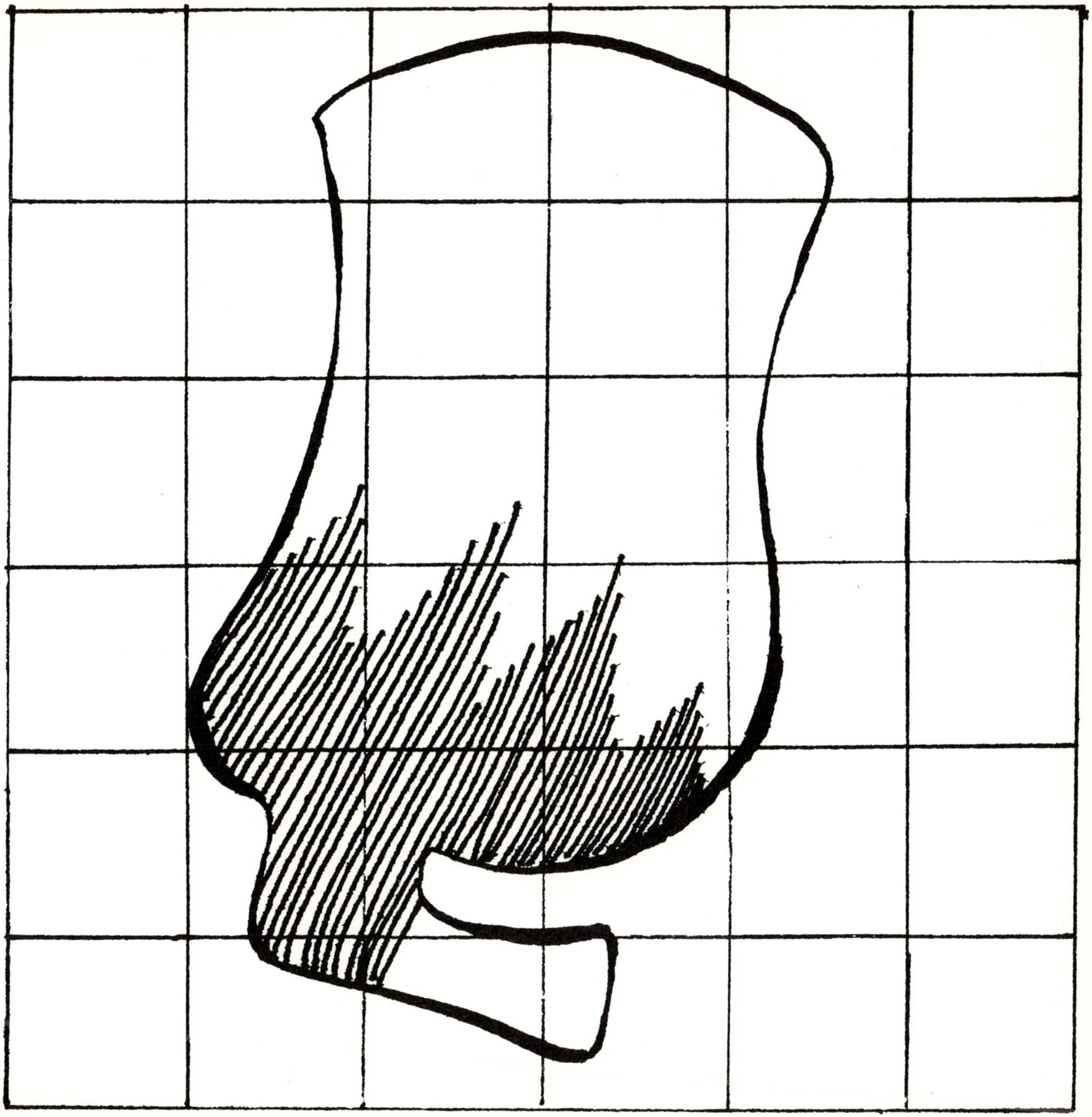

METHOD

Make a tracing paper pattern from the graph on the previous page.

Cut out the pattern and use it as a template to cut eight petals from the red paper.

Draw in the decoration at the base of each petal with the black felt pen.

Curl each petal so that it curves in an S shape.

Wind the base of the petals round the tip of the wire one at a time. Fix each one with masking tape as you go, overlapping the petals. Finally bind all eight firmly at the base with the tape and paint the tape with red ink to match. Bind the stem with crêpe paper, glued into position.

Cartridge paper art deco daisy

MATERIALS

A piece of thick wire 354 mm (14 in.) long, or a split bamboo stick of the same length
One sheet of cartridge paper
Pink, yellow and orange ink
Rubber solution glue
Scissors
A cork
Pencil, graph paper

METHOD

Make a graph paper pattern for each of the shapes given on the graphs shown on the previous page. Cut them out and use as templates.
Cut out shapes A, B and C from the cartridge paper and paint them with the inks in the patterns shown on the graphs.
Curl up the petals by pulling them between the thumb and the blunt side of the scissors.
Glue the centre back of shape C to the centre front of shape B. Then glue the centre back of shape B to the centre front of shape A.
Cut the cork in half and glue one half to the centre back of shape A.
Drive the tip of the stem into the cork.

Cartridge paper art deco daisy

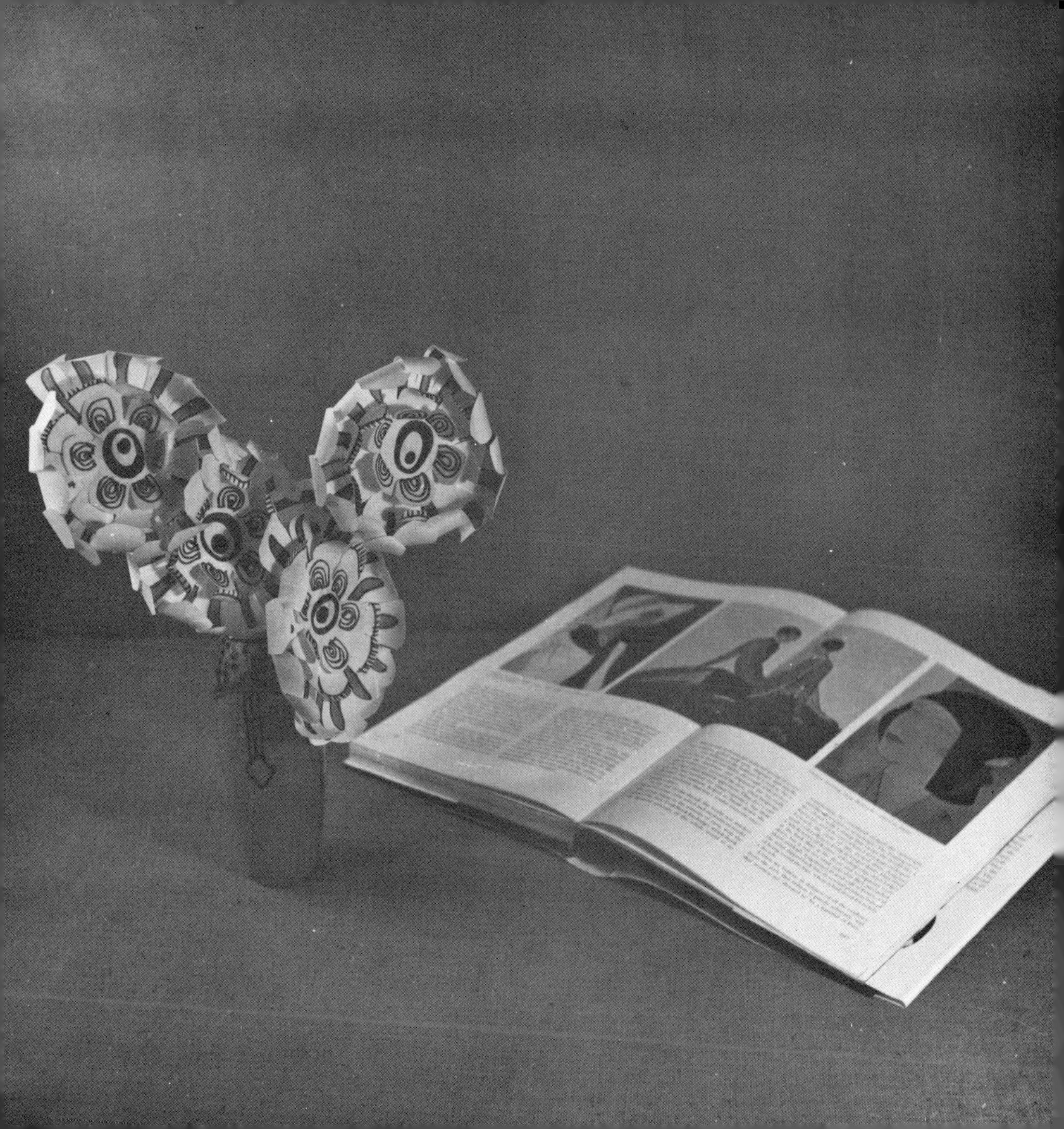

MIXED PAPER FLOWERS

INTRODUCTION

While crêpe, tissue and cartridge paper are all extremely effective for flower making, there are several other papers that give scope for ideas.
Brown wrapping paper has a faint grain and the added advantage of one shiny side and one dull side, this gives surface interest.
Paper doilies, with their pierced surface look particularly effective, and even hard and heavy papers such as sandpaper can look interesting if allied with a paper that gives a contrasting surface.
Many of the flowers given in the cartridge and tissue section will adapt to brown paper, cellophane or tin foil (the crêpe paper flowers usually need stretching and this is impossible with a firm paper).

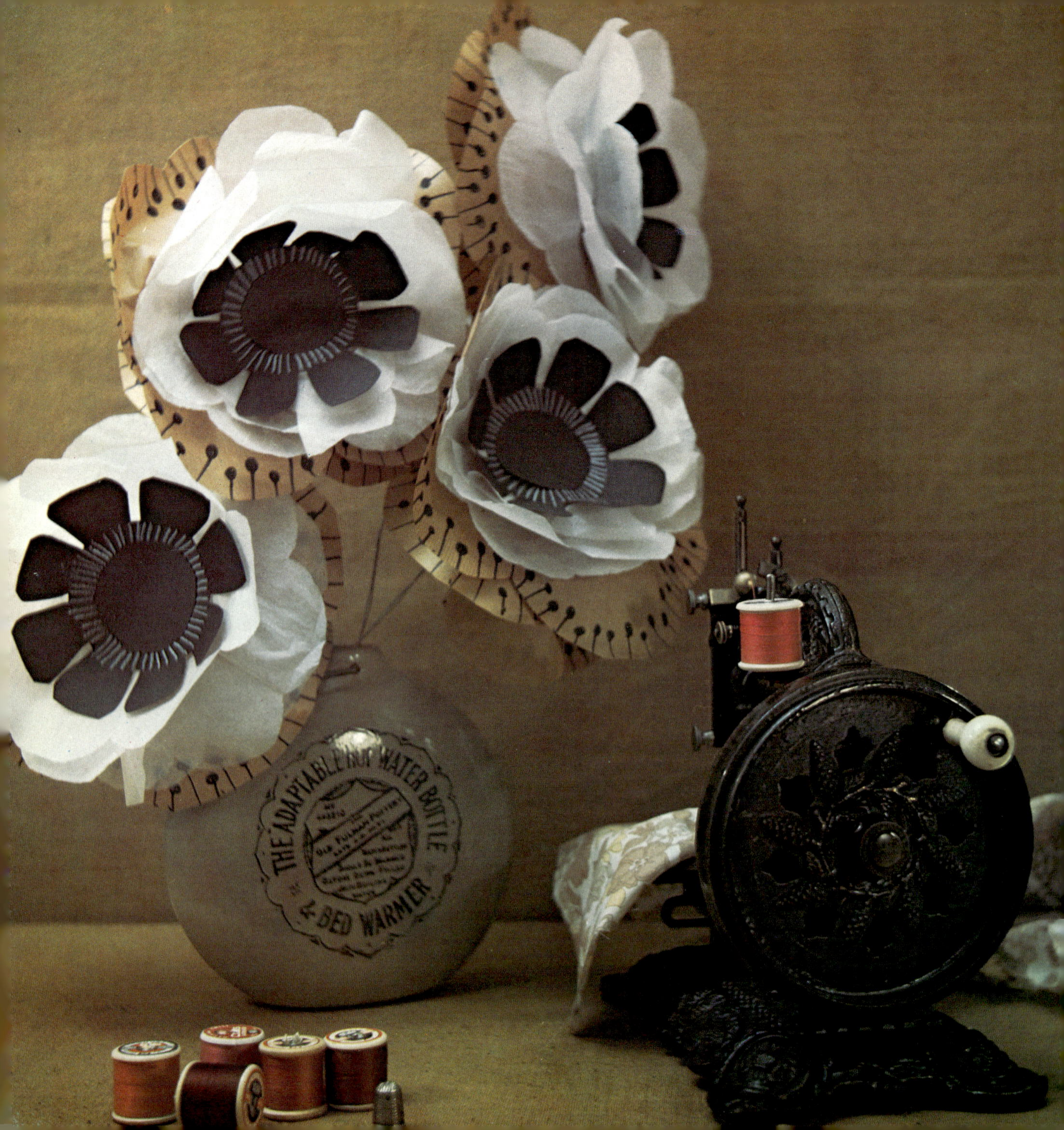
THE ADAPTABLE HOT WATER BOTTLE
& BED WARMER

Mixed paper flower 1

MATERIALS

A piece of thick wire 431 mm (17 in.) long, or a split bamboo stick of the same length
One sheet of brown wrapping paper
One sheet of black cartridge paper
One sheet of white tissue paper
Rubber solution glue
Scissors
Yellow or white wax crayon (or paint)
Pencil, graph paper 25 mm (1 in.) squares, black felt tip pen

PLATE 4 *(Opposite)*   *Mixed paper flower 1*

METHOD

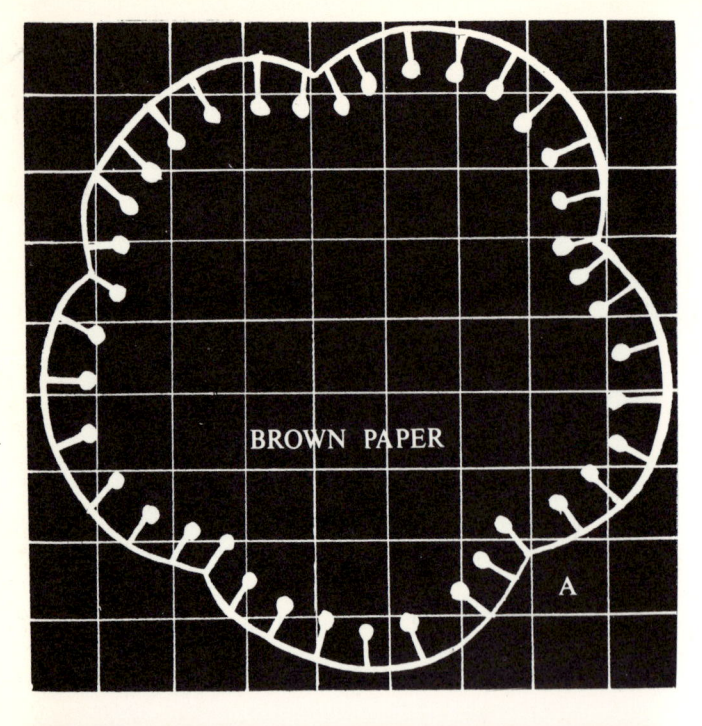

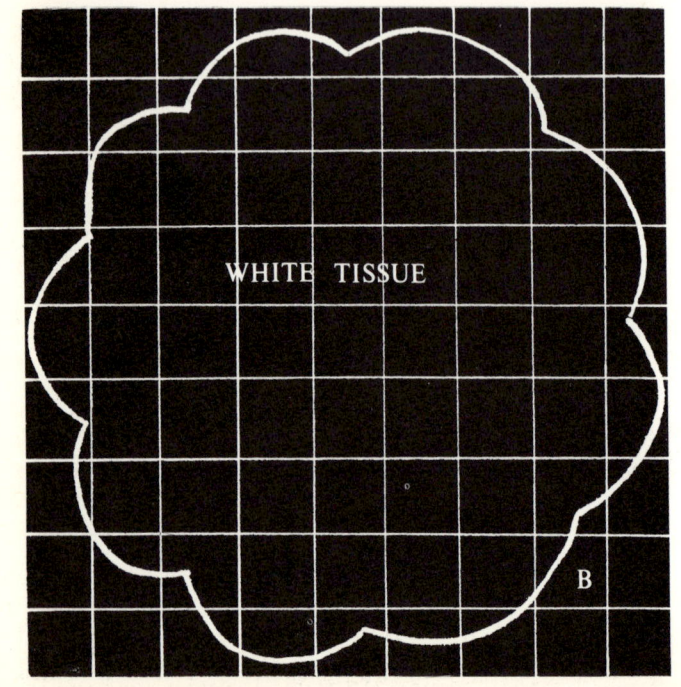

Make paper patterns for shapes A, B and C [one square on the graph is equal to 25 mm (1 in.)]. Cut out the patterns.

Using the patterns as templates, cut four shapes A from brown wrapping paper, six shapes B from white tissue and three shapes C from black cartridge paper. Decorate the brown paper shapes with the black felt pen and the black paper ones with the wax crayons or paint.

Put a dab of glue onto the centre back of a shape A and push the end of the thick wire stem through the centre of the shape so that it protrudes for about 12 mm ($\frac{1}{2}$ in.). Hold the paper with the finger tips of one hand and the wire in the other. Give the paper a sharp twist so that it is slightly gathered round the stem.

Add the other brown paper shapes behind the first. Push the tip of the stem through the centre of the tissue paper shapes B and glue and twist them as for the shapes A.

Push the tip of the stem through the black paper shapes C, adding a dab of glue to hold them firmly.

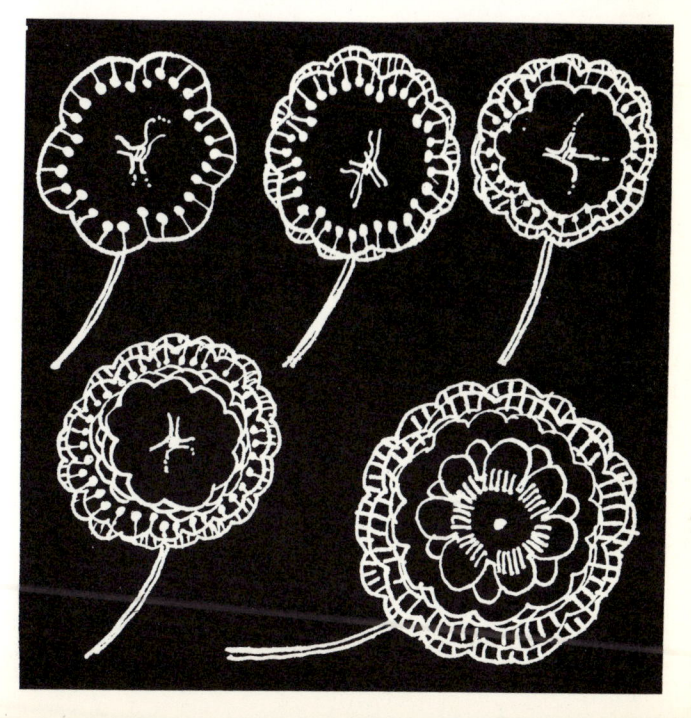

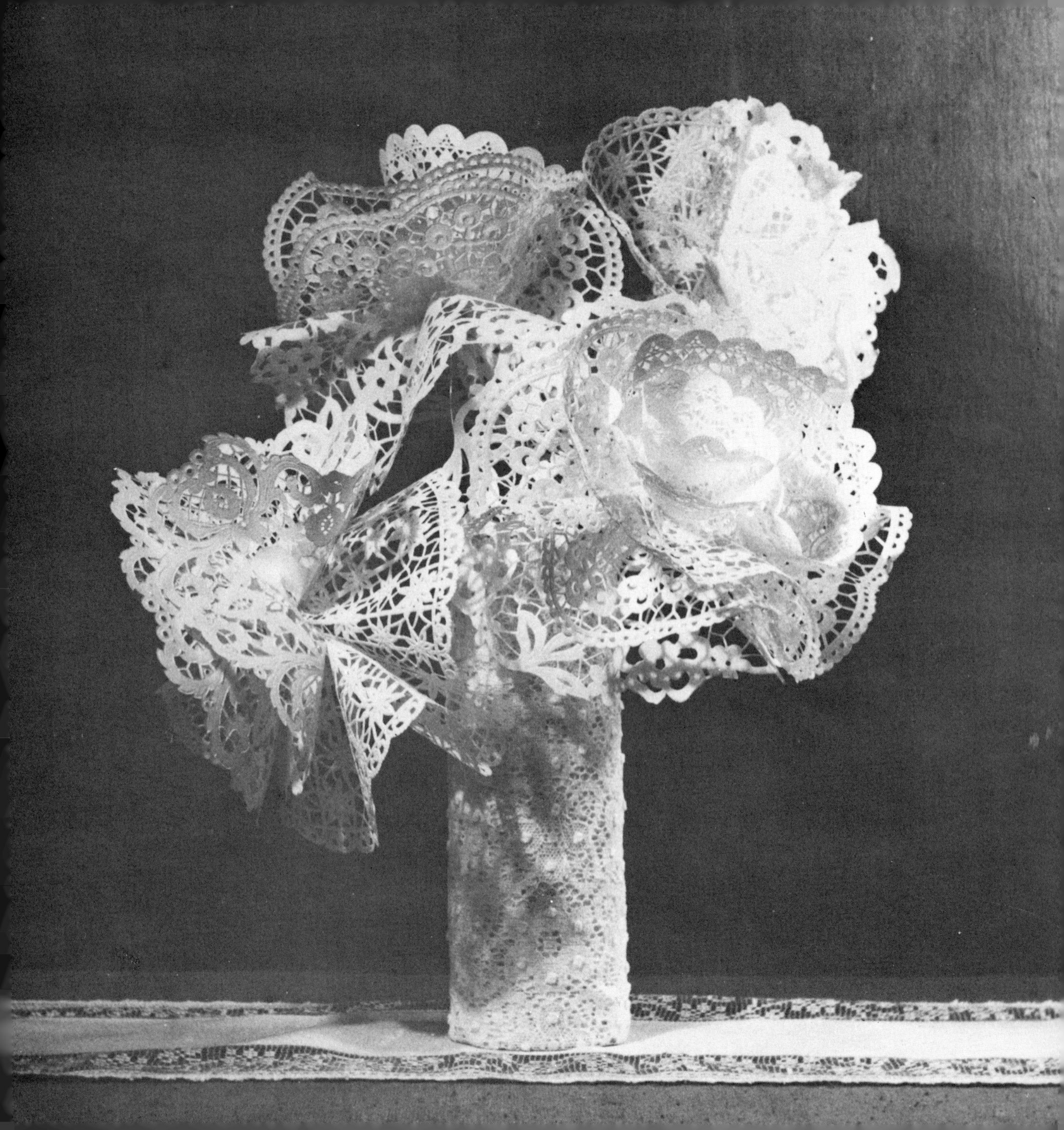

Mixed paper flower 2

MATERIALS

Three doilies in either white, silver or gold
A piece of medium weight wire 381 mm (15 in.) long
Rubber solution glue

METHOD

Push the tip of the wire through the centre of the first doily, put a dab of glue onto the tip of the stem and pinch the centre of the doily round this.
Push the next doily onto the tip of the stem and add another dab of glue and pinch the doily round the stem again.
Add the third doily in the same way and pinch the centre so that the tip of the stem is hidden.

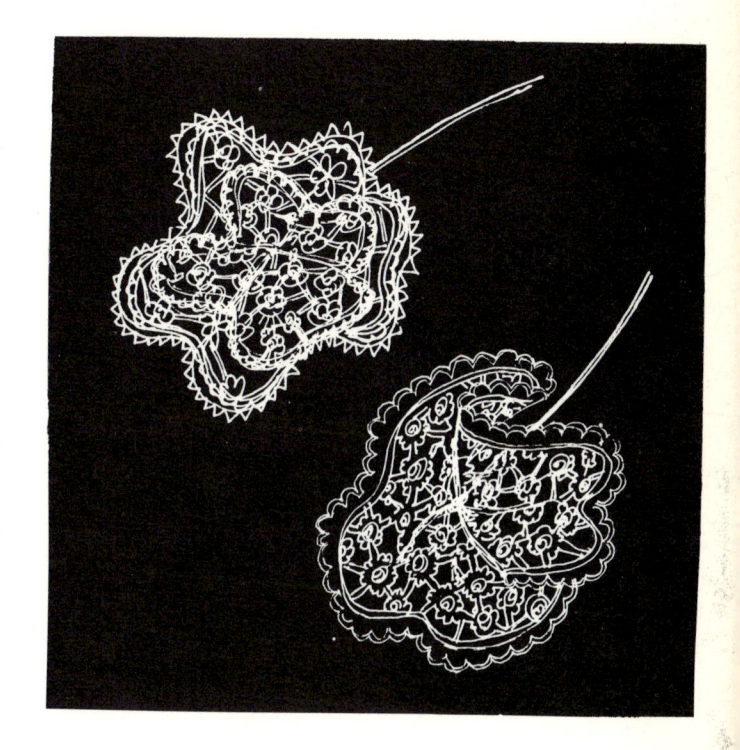

Mixed paper flower 2

WREATHS AND DECORATIONS

INTRODUCTION

There are many ways of using the finished flowers, from simple arrangements of massed flowers to more sophisticated arrangements with dried grasses and plants. Flowers can be joined together on a stiff wire circle to form wreaths or table decorations, or strung on a flexible thread to make garlands and necklaces. A formal arrangement of simple flowers can be anchored with *Plasticine* or set into a glass flower holder.
Twenty or thirty tiny flowers can be fixed to a polystyrene wig stand to decorate a dressing table, or a bunch of blooms can be fixed to a wrapped gift.
If a thin wire stem is used the flowers will sway slightly, and a thick wire stem can be bent and so give complicated but firm arrangements. The possibilities for arrangement and invention are almost endless, and with a little ingenuity a wide range of individual and highly decorative effects can be achieved.

Christmas wreath

MATERIALS

At least 1·8 m (6 feet) of medium weight wire in a continuous strand
About sixty pieces of medium wire each 203 mm (8 in.) long
912 mm (1 yard) of red satin ribbon 25 mm (1 in.) wide
Two packets of dark green crêpe paper
One packet of red crêpe paper
One packet of white crêpe paper
Rubber solution glue
Scissors
Pencil, graph paper 25 mm (1 in.) squares

METHOD

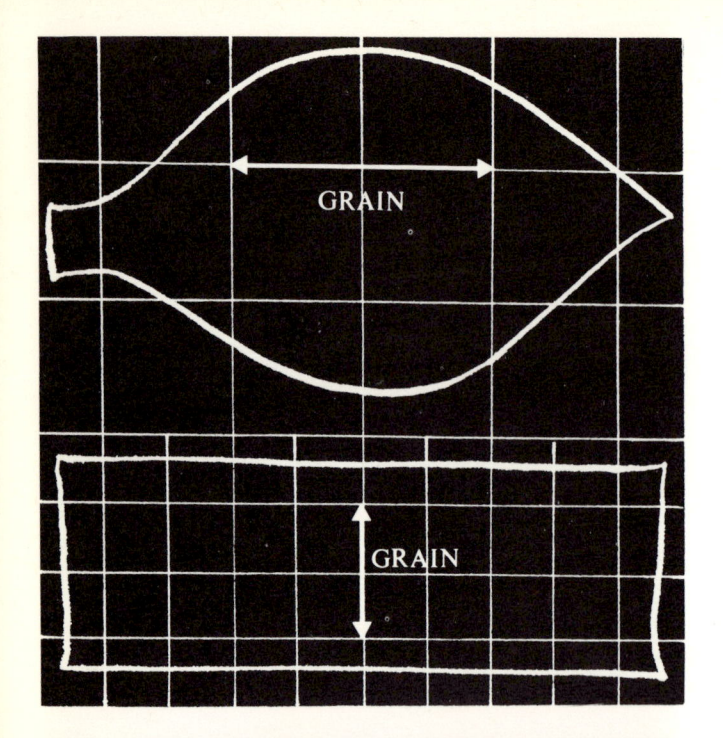

Wind the long strand of wire into a circle, three strands thick, twisting them together. Tuck the ends in so that they are secure.

Make a graph paper pattern for the leaves [one square on the graph is equal to 25 mm (1 in.)]. Cut the pattern out and use it as a template to cut thirty leaves from the green crêpe paper.

Make twenty red flowers and ten white as for the crêpe flower posy on page 37. Make the stems from the 203 mm (8 in.) lengths of wire.

Glue the bases of the leaves onto the stems at the base of the flowers. Twist the stems onto the wire circle, tucking the ends inside the circle. Arrange the flower heads so that they stand out from the leaves. It may be necessary to make more leaves to fill in any spaces.

IDEAS FOR WREATHS

(a) Silver foil roses and leaves wound round the circle of wire
(b) Tiny tissue paper poppies with christmas tree glass decorations
(c) White cartridge paper daisies and tinsel

Christmas wreaths

89

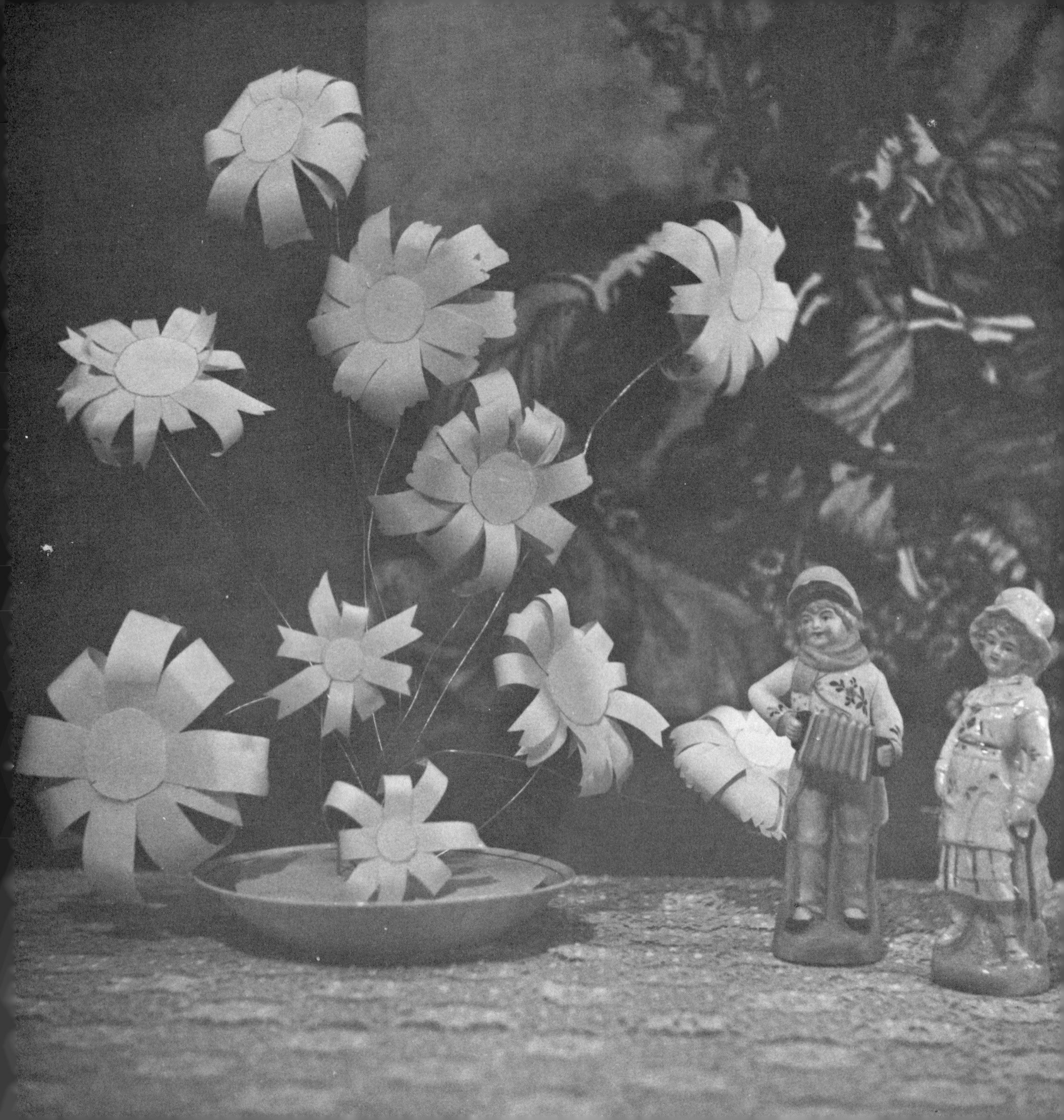

Dish arrangement

MATERIALS

One sheet of white cartridge paper
Yellow, orange, carmine and pink inks
Paint brush
Green crêpe paper
Eight 354 mm (14 in.) lengths of medium weight wire
(heavy fuse wire is excellent)
Rubber solution glue
Scissors
Plasticine (a fairly large lump)
Three corks cut into quarters
Pencil, graph paper 25 mm (1 in.) squares

Dish arrangement

METHOD

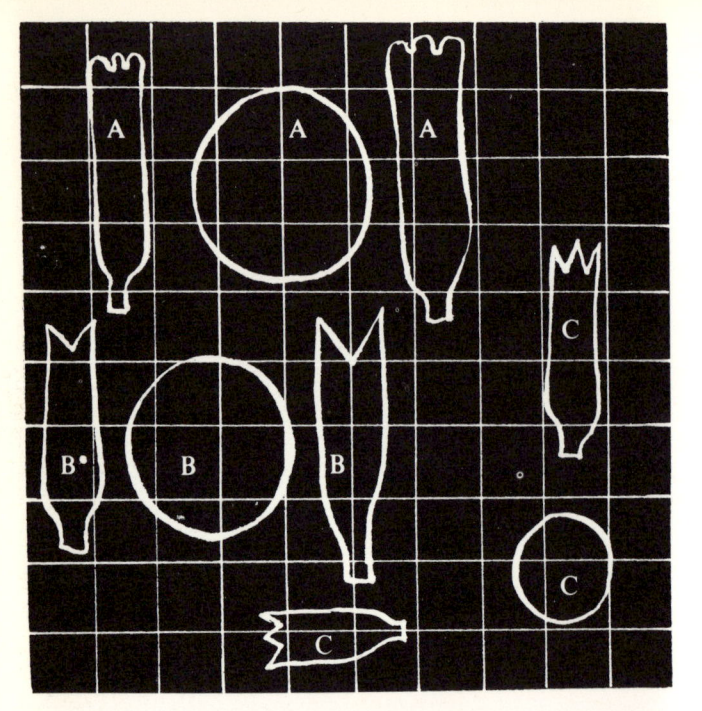

Make graph paper patterns for all the shapes on the graph [one square equals 25 mm (1 in.)].
Cut out the patterns and use them as templates to draw the shapes onto the white cartridge paper. Draw eight petals in each shape and two circles in each size.
Paint all the circles yellow, shapes A are orange, shapes B are carmine and shapes C pink.
Make the flowers up as for the daisy on page 72.
Stick the cork pieces onto the back of each flower and drive the tip of the wire stem into the cork.
The other ends of the wire are pushed into the lump of *Plasticine* which is concealed by green crêpe paper, and stand the *Plasticine* in a shallow dish.
These flowers need not be painted. They look very effective in white only.

Cornucopia

MATERIALS

Two sheets of white cartridge paper
Eight 152 mm (6 in.) lengths of medium wire
Two corks cut into quarters
Rubber solution glue
Coloured inks
Scissors
Newspaper
A needle and thread
Pencil, graph paper 25 mm (1 in.) squares

METHOD

Make graph paper patterns for all the shapes given in the graphs on this and the previous page [one square on the graph equals 25 mm (1 in.)]
Cut the patterns out and use them as templates to cut out at least ten of each shape.
Paint the patterns with the coloured inks on the shapes as shown on the graphs.

To assemble the flowers and cone

Flower A: Stick *a* to *b*, *b* to *c* and *c* to *d*.
Flower B: Stick *a* to *b*, *b* to *c*.
Cone: Bend the unused sheet of card round to form a cone. Glue the edges to hold firmly. Trim the top edge level. Crumple the newspaper and push it down inside the cone.
Glue the pieces of cork to the back of eight flowers, drive the wire into the corks and push the other end into the crumpled newspaper. Arrange the flowers to hide the newspaper and so that they show above the edge of the cone. Make flower chains with the needle and thread, about four flowers on each thread. Sew these chains to the edge of the cone and let them trail. To make a holder for the cone, use medium wire twisted into a loop and fit the cone into it. The other ends are twisted into a hook which can then be hung from a picture hook.

Cornucopia

SUPPLIERS

PAPERS AND COLOURING MATERIALS

Fred Aldous Limited
The Handicrafts Centre
37 Lever Street
Manchester M60 1UX

E. J. Arnold (School Suppliers)
Butterley Street
Leeds LS10 1AX

Arts and Crafts
10 Byram Street
Huddersfield HD1 1DA

Crafts Unlimited
Macklin Street, London WC2

Dennison Manufacturing Company Ltd
Colonial Way
Watford, Herts *(Crêpe paper)*

Dryad Ltd
Northgates, Leicester

Nottingham Handcrafts Company (School Suppliers)
Melton Road
West Bridgeford
Nottingham

Paperchase Products Ltd
216 Tottenham Court Road, London W1

George Rowney and Company Ltd
10 Percy Street, London W1

Winsor and Newton Ltd
Wealdstone
Harrow, Middx *(and branches)*

Reeves and Sons Ltd
Lincoln Road
Enfield, Middx *(and branches)*

Also most stationers, hardware shops, general stores and artists colourmen

WIRE, FUSE WIRE, BAMBOO STICKS, GLUE

Hardware shops and most branches of *Woolworth Ltd*